Finding The One

Finding The One

A Practical Guide to Manifesting Your Soul Mate

Rachel Blacker

Copyright © 2022 by Rachel Blacker

All rights reserved.
No part of this book may be reproduced in any form or by any electronic or mechanical means, including information storage and retrieval systems, without written permission from the author, except for the use of brief quotations in a book review.

First edition June 2022

Cover design by Charlie Blacker

ISBN 978-0-6455191-3-6 (hardback)
ISBN 978-0-6455191-0-5 (ebook)
ISBN 978-0-6455191-1-2 (paperback)
ISBN 978-0-6455191-2-9 (audiobook)

Published by Soul Connect Publishing
www.rachelblacker.com.au

In loving memory of Sally

For CHARLIE BLACKER

I began 'writing' this book long before I met you. You have inspired me, believed in me and supported me at every step. Without you, this book would not have been possible. My eternal appreciation to you, my love.

For DAD

You are one of the most intelligent, gentle, kind, creative and open-minded souls I have ever known. I am proud of you always and honoured to be your daughter.

And for YOU

My dear reader, without your desire for great love, this book would not have been born. In deepest appreciation to you. May you have many blessings in life and in love.

All that you need is within you.
As you realise your true perfection,
you manifest a most divine union.

Contents

Introduction	13
1. Believe in the Existence of Your Ideal Partner	21
2. Decide Exactly What You Want	25
3. Keep Your Heart Open	33
4. Be the Person You Wish to Be	49
5. Discover Your Worth	55
6. Don't Settle for Second Best	61
7. Find Completeness Within	67
8. Fall in Love with Life	73
9. Let Go and Trust	79
10. How to Let Go and Trust	85
11. Practice Appreciation	91
12. Affirmations	99
13. Meditation	107
14. Take Care of Yourself and Your Appearance	117
15. Live Your Life as You Imagine it to be with Your Ideal Partner	125
16. Falling in Love is Just Chemicals in Your Bloodstream	131
17. Take Up a Hobby that You Love	137
18. Don't be Afraid to Say a Quality 'No'	143
19. Forget About Meeting Your Soul Mate!	149
20. Foster Positive Friendships	155
21. Coping with Rejection	161
22. Observe Other Couples and Relationships	169
23. Rectify Negative Self-Talk	173
24. Set Them Free	179

25. Ask Yourself 'Why Do I want to Meet the One?'	185
26. Enjoy Being Single	191
27. Life After Meeting 'the One'	197
About the Author	203
Recommended Resources	205

Introduction

At the age of eighteen, I was dating a boy. It somehow didn't feel ideal, even though he was handsome with dark skin, brown eyes and brown hair, the way I had always fantasised. He was fit and healthy and I knew he would make a dedicated husband someday. But something was amiss.

As a big believer in dream interpretation, I decided to ask my dreams for guidance. I would go to bed every night and ask, 'is he the one?' Frustratingly, my dreams were nothing but mind chatter; useless, weird symbolism that hardly made any sense at all. Until one morning, just prior to awakening, I had a dream that would haunt me for years to come.

My dream began only with the sound of static but then it became apparent that I was listening to the sound of a radio dial tuning between different stations, occasionally picking up signals. At each stop of the dial, there was a station broadcasting an urgent news bulletin. The sound waves were full of reports that the end of the world was imminent.

The magnetic poles of the earth were showing signs they were about to suddenly reverse. 'East was meeting West.' It was to be the end of the world as we knew it. Oddly, there were lots of people looting and trashing local buildings and shops. I thought that this was a bizarre thing to do considering that once we have passed from this Earth, there is nothing material that we can take with us.

I had a sudden realisation; the only thing that had ever been important, that will ever be important, is love. At that instant, all became silent and still. I found myself in a state of extreme presence, feeling deep peace and gazing at an extraordinary scene whilst sitting atop a large sandstone rock that was just offshore in the ocean.

I had my attention fixed on the horizon, watching and waiting. It was warm, yet overcast and the sea was calm. There were storm clouds forming in the distance. I could sense the electricity in the air, as though something magical was coming. I became spooked for no apparent reason and a wave, as if sensing my fear, crashed up onto the rock, narrowly missing me as it receded back into the ocean.

I turned to my left and there he was; a young boy just sitting there on the rock gazing at me. He was handsome. He had olive skin, short blonde hair and blue eyes. Our eyes met and we both knew. Without uttering a single word, there was a powerful knowing that this was the man who was perfect for me in every way. The attraction was instant.

Unanimously, we turned back to face the shore, climbed down from the rock and entered the rock pool that lay between us and the shore. We swam together in the still, aqua-coloured, crystal-clear water, in the most blissful and sensual experience I had ever known.

When we reached the shore, we simply lay there on the sand, content to stare into one another's eyes. I had the sense that not all was perfect with the world but now that we had found one another, nothing would ever be the same again.

When I woke up, I knew my boyfriend was not the one for me and I knew that my blonde-haired, blue-eyed, olive-skinned boy would one day find me and at just the right time. I knew I need not concern myself with when, how or where we would meet. Our meeting would simply come to pass and at precisely the right time.

That was how I felt immediately after I woke up. But then the memory of the dream faded. I stayed with my boyfriend at the time for a total of two years. Towards the end, we had grown apart. To many people in our lives, we looked like the perfect couple but something just wasn't right.

My heart was no longer in the relationship and I didn't know why. It was only years later that I realised the many reasons for this feeling. He didn't share my sense of adventure and connection to nature. He was a very content person and happy to just sail by in life but I needed something more, even though I wasn't precisely sure what it was.

So, I ended our relationship and set myself free, I thought, to be with the boy from my dream. I always kept a lookout for him. I was always on alert because maybe I would bump into him on the street. What if he passed me by and I didn't notice him? And when? When would he be coming?

Every once in a while, I would meet someone special and those blissful, sensual feelings would flow and I would think, 'It's him! I've found him!' only to realise that the person didn't love me and that the moment of bliss was fleeting.

It took me a very long time to work out that perhaps not all men had the same intentions and desires as I did. I felt hurt and betrayed. There were even times when I doubted my dream and the existence of the boy from my dream; 'What if it was just a dream? Why do I believe in a dream? Is he really real?'

There were times when I felt like a complete lunatic and other times when I became cynical, criticising my desire. But I didn't give up hope altogether. I let go of my tenacious grip on my dream of 'the one' but I always had a certain amount of hope it would one day come to pass that this man would enter my life.

Introduction

As the years went by and I became older and older, I started to accept that perhaps I wouldn't find him until well after my childbearing years. I would acknowledge the thought and let it go. 'It will all work out somehow,' I thought. Nevertheless, I refused to compromise by being with a man who wasn't right for me.

I had a strong need for affection and so I dated some incredible people but there was a powerful and intuitive part of me that made me feel almost physically ill if I had spent too much time with the 'wrong' person. I grew to love being alone. In fact, I fell in love with life and with my own company.

And that is precisely when I found him. At the age of thirty-four, I was so appreciative that I didn't find him any sooner. As it turns out, he really was a boy when I first encountered him once upon a dream. The man of my dreams is eleven years younger than me! And so, the timing of the Universe was absolutely perfect. We met at just the right time. I had finally grown enough to be a person that I loved and could be proud of. I finally felt worthy of the love of a lifetime. I finally felt complete all on my own.

In the time that I remained single, my faith came and went. There were times of doubt when I considered settling down with some nice man so that I could just marry, purchase a house and have kids; the way that most of my peers had done. But my feelings of intuition were too strong.

Introduction

Often there was something inside of me just screaming out 'Don't do it!' And I remained single and found that I was, in fact, deeply satisfied alone. There was even a time when I would question whether I could be happy in the company of another, as I enjoyed being alone so much! But eventually, I did find the boy from my dream and I do enjoy his company as much as I enjoy being alone, so it has all worked out perfectly.

I am so happy I didn't settle for somebody who was not the boy from my dream. But what if I had? What if I had compromised my desires and chosen a mate based on what I felt society expected of me? What if I had just 'taken the plunge' and committed to being with a man, purely on the basis of chemistry? What if we weren't really compatible once the chemistry had worn off and we ended up in a loveless marriage trying to resurrect that initial feeling of attraction and euphoria that was there in the beginning? What if we had gone through the motions of traditional milestones, such as getting engaged, married or having children, in the hope that these things would bring the happiness that we had been promised in Hollywood films? What if I remained committed to this man, all the while recognising his potential to be the man of my dreams and hoping that I could change him, oblivious to the futility of such a task? Would going to couples counselling, seminars and workshops be enough to save our dying marriage; a union that was initially intended for life? What if I had given up hope, given in to cynicism and

Introduction

stopped believing in the possibility of finding a partner who is compatible on multiple levels?

While I could have taken this path, as so many do, I chose instead to tenaciously believe in a dream with no evidence that it was the right choice. This choice seemed crazy to me on a number of occasions, however, with the gift of hindsight, I could not be happier with this decision.

At the end of the day, a failing marriage, while difficult and upsetting for all involved, isn't the end of the world. There is no right or wrong in life. There is only a reflection of your truest desires and the continual creation of who you are now and who you are becoming. The degree to which your life reflects this truth largely depends on how honest you are with yourself.

I really wanted to know myself and learn what would make me happy within the context of a romantic relationship to give it the best chance of being a satisfying, joyful and harmonious union. So, the question here is, which path do you wish to follow? Are you a person who believes in an extraordinary romantic relationship that can enhance your life and bring it to greater heights of love than you had ever imagined possible?

If this is you and if you do believe or at least hope that your other half does exist, if you are surrounded by cynics and sceptics and need a fresh injection of positive energy to boost you in the direction towards your dreams, then you have come to exactly the right place.

Chapter 1

Believe in the Existence of Your Ideal Partner

On your quest for love, it will serve you well to hold the belief that there is somebody out there who is absolutely perfect for you. I know that because you are reading this, there is already a part of you that is, at the very least, hopeful. But now it is time to either begin believing or to bring your belief to the surface and into your conscious awareness.

This belief is a critical first step. While desire alone may be enough for your ideal partner to show up in your experience, it is much less likely without belief. This is because not believing in your ideal partner is likely to negatively influence the types of people who enter your experience and/or cause you to ignore evidence that points to exactly what it is that you wish for.

I had a feeling growing up (although I didn't always believe in it) that somewhere out there, was a boy also wishing for and hoping to find me. It turns out that at this point in time, he wasn't even born yet! So, I wonder sometimes, did the Universe make him just for me because honestly, he complements me perfectly!

Just as a side note here, I would like to point out that many people are uncomfortable with the word 'perfect' because it can imply 'without fault.' Since we are all growing and evolving as human beings, then being 'faultless' isn't possible, especially in retrospect, when we become aware of better ways to approach life. However, my understanding of the word 'perfect' and the way that I use it here, is more along the lines of 'ideal', meaning that a situation, thing or person is suitable for you in every respect, in terms of what you say you wish to achieve.

In a romantic relationship, it is possible to find your ideal, given what you say you want the relationship to achieve and you can find somebody who complements you on multiple levels. But we will explore this in more detail in the next chapter.

Believing in my perfect partner was challenging for me during my formative years, as I did not have examples of wholesome love relationships in my life. All of the partnerships I had seen modelled by my family were amicable at best but they were not remarkable in a positive sense.

In my own household, there were many arguments and great love was also associated with great conflict, violence and pain. I often fantasised about a perfect partner but I had no idea if it was just a fantasy or exactly what this fantasy might look like, should it come into existence.

Believe in the Existence of Your Ideal Partner

It will be helpful for you to believe in your ideal partner, regardless of whether you have examples of this in your life. As I grew much older and had more experience with dating, I decided to just believe in what I wanted, regardless of whether I had evidence for it. As soon as I had made this decision, miracles started occurring in my life.

What you will find is that there are actually examples of the very thing you wish to create that exist in the world already. And as you start to toy with the idea of this perfect person, you will look for and find examples proving the very thing that you wish to create. Your perspective will naturally begin to alter and you will notice things, even small things, that you may have previously overlooked.

Very early on, after I had made my decision to believe in my ideal partner, I happened upon a book that was just the thing I needed to shore up my faith. It is called 'Hot Chocolate for the Mystical Soul' by Arielle Ford and it is a collection of short stories of a mystical nature, some of which are uplifting romance stories of soul mates and preordained relationships.

I couldn't believe my luck in stumbling upon this book! These were real-life examples of the very thing I wished to find in my life! I had goose bumps and tears welling up as I read some of the heart-warming tales of lovers united and I became really inspired.

Although I always had some hope of the existence of my soul mate, I actually started to believe! Maybe I wasn't crazy after all! Maybe it was okay to believe in my dream, or rather, my 'premonition,' as I began calling it.

If you are having difficulty believing in your ideal or if you are too frightened to trust that something better can come along, then it won't be possible or conducive to force yourself to do so. Instead, it will be beneficial for you to intend to see examples of this in your life. And this will happen without a doubt.

Simply set the intention 'I would like to believe in my ideal partner (or ideal relationship)' and then be happy, be present and be observant. The examples will begin to make themselves apparent to you. When you see these examples of great love relationships or qualities that you admire in others, be sure to acknowledge them and give your appreciation to the Universe and to yourself, for your powerful creative abilities.

Your appreciation, even of little signs and signals, will be essential to bringing your ideal partner into your life. Appreciation will top you up to the brim with joy and completeness in acknowledgement of all that you already have and this is the very energy that will bring more of what you wish for to you. Believe in the existence of your ideal partner and honour the manifestations that occur thereafter.

Chapter 2

Decide Exactly What You Want

While I don't consider it to be necessary to date a stupendous number of people in order to find your perfect partner, I found that having extensive dating experience was very helpful to me in identifying my preferences.

If you don't wish to date a lot of people, this is also fine. In this instance, simply being observant of individual people, couples and friends in your life can provide you with enough data to determine what you do and don't wish for in a romantic relationship.

Being astute in your observation of others can assist you in recognising exactly what it is that you're looking for when it does come into your life. Alternatively, having a rich dating life (or interviewing friends who do) can also provide you with some valuable insights.

Although my dating history may have been rather chaotic at times, I believe in extracting the absolute best out of all of my past experiences and so I have gained a veritable wealth of knowledge. As I mentioned earlier, I didn't have many examples of successful romantic relationships in my life and so the best part of my dating experience was that I was able to home in on exactly what I found desirable and undesirable in a romantic partner and relationship.

So, when my life coach instructed me to write a list of one hundred traits I would like to see in my ideal partner, it was surprisingly easy. When considering dating any future 'applicants,' I was advised that the person must satisfy ninety percent of my criteria and there were to be no 'deal-breakers.' For example, if they were a cigarette smoker, it was a deal-breaker for me.

When you are deciding what you want, it is important to honour what is in your heart and what really turns you on. We're talking about your ideal partner here! This isn't somebody you're just settling for because you're being 'realistic' or don't believe that you can do any better because of poor self-esteem or scarcity beliefs. This is somebody who excites you! This is somebody you're excited to meet and to be with, along with all of the other sensible things that you may wish for, such as somebody who is genuine and trustworthy. You also want them to be attractive and you want them to be attracted to you and in love with you unconditionally!

Don't be afraid to address physical appearance and physical attributes. If you are a short man and you're attracted to tall and slender ladies, then you need to honour this! Chances are that this desire isn't superficial; you may simply have an intuition that the woman of your dreams just happens to be tall and slender and if she is the one for you, then it means that you are her ideal as well.

If a certain physical appearance matters to you, then you need to add this to your list. It may not be a deal-breaker for you if your partner doesn't have blonde hair, for example but it is nice to add it all the same, just to paint a picture.

It is worthwhile mentioning here that every person has different preferences. There is no one ideal look (despite what we are being told by the fashion industry) and every person will be drawn to their own unique set of characteristics.

I am well aware that I am stating the obvious but this is deliberate, as I have heard far too many people forget this simple fact and belittle themselves because they don't believe that they are attractive due to their looks. Attractiveness isn't only about how you look. Even so, it may surprise you to discover that your particular look may be exactly what your ideal person has been hoping to find. Appreciate your uniqueness! There are so many complexities that make humans unique and individual preferences are just as varied.

I really want this point to sink in; do not sell yourself short because you don't think you are attractive! There is a specific individual on this planet for whom your own brand of uniqueness is exactly what *they* are looking for!

Start thinking about what it is that *you* want. Not what you think you should settle for based on scarcity thinking or not feeling worthy. Decide exactly what it is that *you* like; not what society tells you that you should like but what you actually like.

In writing your list, you are describing your very own person, a person who suits you perfectly. You won't be describing my perfect person or the perfect person of a friend of yours. You will be describing your own set of special characteristics that are an ideal match for you. It isn't selfish or unrealistic to decide exactly what you want in another human being and to hold out for that special someone.

I will admit that after sixteen years of waiting for my ideal partner to come into my life, there were times when I asked myself 'Am I being too fussy? Am I being unrealistic?' But then the Universe stepped in with signs that I was on the right path, in the form of meeting men who were almost everything that I wanted.

I met him in various forms and at one point, I wished that if I could take this guy's good looks and combine it with that guy's love of surfing and that other guy's maturity and spiritual awareness and all the rest, I could have my perfect guy; a kind of Mr Potato Head cut-and-paste version of my perfect man.

Eventually, I met only one man with everything I wished for and the best part is that my man is one hundred percent of my list of criteria and better still, he is more than all of the things I put on my list and even the surprising things I had only ever dared to whisper in my dreams.

In putting together a list of your ideal partner, essentially you are looking at the types of people who are available to you and choosing what it is that you like about them. This will help you to see your dream of your ideal partner coming to life all around you. When you can imagine and get a feeling for what it is that you want, you are in a much better position to manifest it into your life.

Maybe you like the way you feel at ease around your ideal person. Maybe you like that you can be silly and laugh together. You may wish to share similar spiritual beliefs. Perhaps you appreciate how your partner helps you grow emotionally and spiritually. You could write an endless list if you want to!

Be honest with yourself about what it is that you really want in your heart. Your list will help to make sure that you don't compromise and that you stay true to yourself and what it is that you desire.

There are also some really significant questions to ask yourself at this point in time. Am I the person I want to be? Do I reflect my heart's truest desires? And if I met this person tomorrow, am I ready to receive such a person into my life?

You don't have to consider yourself to be perfect because your ideal partner will see you as perfect no matter what. But you do need to love yourself to a certain extent and start living your life as you would if your perfect person was already a part of your life. We will go into detail on this a little later.

I have heard many people sprout the eargasm 'Nobody can love you unless you love yourself.' This may sound sensible at first, that is, until you actually think about it. I know of many instances where people do not love themselves but are doted upon and adored by a spouse, parent, grandparent, friend, sibling and so on.

You do not need to love yourself to be loved by another. But loving yourself will help you be aware of and appreciate the love of another; in other words, it will help you to receive love. It will also put you in a healthy position of not *needing* love and therefore, will result in a thriving, interdependent (rather than co-dependent) relationship when the time comes.

One thing that I would like to mention here is that when you write your list, you may find that your list, to a large extent, reflects who *you* are. I have friends who both wrote lists before they finally met and fell in love with each other. They had instructed me to write a list as well. They pointed out that upon reading both of their lists, they had each described themselves!

While my list had a lot of similarities with me, I also requested some differences. I didn't want to date someone exactly the same as myself and my partner is definitely not exactly the same as me. But we do have a lot of similarities for greater harmony and enough differences to keep challenging, surprising and delighting one another.

Start thinking about what is important to you. Decide what it is that you want in your desired relationship. Begin writing your list of the traits you wish for in your ideal partner. Your list will act as a manifestation aid by helping you to imagine your ideal lover. If you should find yourself becoming delightfully drunk on love, your list will also act as your sober and sensible friend, keeping you in check. Determine what it is that you wish for and then be sure to adhere to your wishes.

Chapter 3

Keep Your Heart Open

If you are putting yourself 'out there' in the dating world and you are reading this, then it means that you probably haven't found 'the one' for you just yet. Chances are you have found a lot of people who are not 'the one.' I was dating and looking for the man of my dreams for sixteen years before I finally found him. This means that in sixteen years, it didn't work out with a single one. I wasn't always the one having my heart broken; I did my fair share of breaking hearts and I learned a lot about break-ups.

I have witnessed many people who have become jaded with the opposite sex (or the same sex) and make them into the enemy. In my time of dating the 'wrong' ones, I realised some very significant things. If something hasn't worked out, it is crucial to be able to let it go and forgive, which means to let go of any inner negativity towards your past lover.

If you are hung up on a past love and finding it difficult to move on, it might be time to be completely honest with yourself. If you consider that a person was perfect for you and you have been pining for them because they have decided that they didn't want to be with you, then the reality is that they aren't perfect for you.

I once met a man who ticked all of the boxes and was 'perfect' in every way but when I started getting to know him, he didn't seem overly keen on me. I thought maybe he hadn't got the message that I was flirting with him, so I ended up blatantly letting him know I was interested. He told me he had a girlfriend.

Before too long, he became single again and once again, I was too late. He had found another girlfriend almost right away! The reality is that he ticked all of the boxes except for one (and that one box was a major deal-breaker); he didn't feel the same way about me as I did about him.

I had to be honest with myself and admit that I had found a guy who was *almost* perfect and move on. I took it as an auspicious sign that what I wanted in a man could exist (he wasn't as rare as a unicorn after all) and thanked the Universe for placing this man on my path.

If you have met someone who is almost perfect but doesn't want to be with you, then they are not really the kind of person you want to be with. It isn't nice trying to persuade somebody to love you or attenuate your behaviour in order to impress a person. If you have to work hard to change your behaviour in order to make sure you don't rub somebody the wrong way or to fit their ideal, if you have to try too hard to make them want you, then are they really perfect for you?

I cannot stress enough how important it is to be honest with yourself if you really want to create change in the future and free yourself for something that is genuinely uplifting and deeply satisfying. It is also really important to soothe and soften your heart towards any of your past relationships. If you can breathe and find a place of stillness within, if you can view your ex-partner through their eyes, if you can be objective and recognise that you don't want somebody who doesn't want you, then you will go a long way towards freeing yourself for the one who *does* want you.

Don't worry about what they did and didn't do. Regardless of what they have done, it is essential that you find a way to forgive them. This doesn't necessarily mean that you condone their behaviour, it doesn't mean that you will have any contact with them but it does mean you will find peace in your heart and do your best to understand their perspective. You will do this so that you won't bring your past hurts and scars into your present and future relationships.

I once had a man in my life who withheld some crucial information from me. Prior to discovering this information, I spent about four months getting to know him and found myself loving him unconditionally. Once I was made privy to this information, I asked him his reason for not revealing the truth to me in the beginning and he stated simply, 'Because if I told the truth, you wouldn't have wanted to know me.' He was right; if I had known the truth, I would have had nothing to do with him. I couldn't argue with his logic but also it was clearly time for the relationship to end.

I wanted to date a man I could trust and one who withholds the truth is not a man I can trust. In all honesty, I don't regret having the opportunity to know him and I understand where he was coming from. He wanted to know me. This was a man who was sweet to his very core but was creating a life of chaos of which I did not wish to be a part. I could have become angry and sprouted sweeping generalisations such as 'men only want one thing' or 'all men are (insert profanity here)' but instead, I forgave him.

I have nothing to do with him now but I am not angry at him and my heart is soft, open and loving. This compassion towards all other human beings is not weakness, nor is it naïve. You can love a person and walk away from them. It takes great strength and courage to allow yourself to be vulnerable emotionally. It is important to foster this gentle and open nature, as it will allow the right person to come to you. If you close and harden your heart, you will block your ability to love and to magnetise love to you.

If you have been treated appallingly in the past and you simply can't forgive your ex-partner, then it may be helpful to stay off the topic and think about something else that is soothing. If you are obsessing over something horrible that somebody did to you and you simply can't let go, then make a decision to change the subject each time the thought or feeling arises. Think of puppies, meditate, take a nap, do some vigorous exercise. Do anything that you need to do in order to feel better.

But it is vital not to make the opposite sex (or your preferred sex) into the enemy. There are many types of different people of all genders. Some people cannot communicate their innermost feelings very well and so finding the truth of their behaviour isn't always possible.

If you are incorrectly jumping to conclusions about people, you will feel terrible angst and anxiety. When you stumble upon the truth, it will always be accompanied by a state of deep peace, or at the very least, a sense of relief.

You can never know for certain what a person thinks and feels but if you are angry at a person, it is because you are judging them and not allowing yourself to see the truth of their actions or to understand the reason behind their actions.

Let's say a person had sex with you and abandoned you. You can look at it in a few different ways. First of all, if it happened, it happened. You can't change that. There is absolutely no point in being angry towards them. Did you have a good time? Did it feel special? Did you think you had a genuine connection? Then there probably was a real connection but for whatever reason, they have decided that you are not right for them or that a relationship with you is not what they would like to pursue.

If you feel used, then this is a lesson to withhold sex until you are sure that being intimate is a risk you are willing to take. It will always be a risk, even if you are married. There is no such thing as forever in this world. Even a lifetime commitment will end once you are deceased. This isn't negativity; it is a simple fact.

So, a person had sex with you and didn't return your calls. At least you know they were not right for you. And at least they chose you! Sharing intimacy with another human being can be one of the most euphoric experiences that life has to offer.

Take it as a compliment that they were drawn to you, even if only for a short while. Take it as a clear sign from the Universe that you are attractive, glowing, on fire and magnetic! Use this experience to your advantage.

Don't try to understand why this person didn't want more than a fling and don't analyse what is wrong with you. Don't let another person dictate your self-esteem and self-worth. There is nothing wrong with you! They just didn't want to be with you and that is okay. This actually works in your favour because you are still free and available for the one who *does* want you.

Keep your heart open. Be forthright with any people you may date. If an experience like this is something you want to avoid, then ask the hard questions. Ask what your date is looking for in a partner. For a long time, I would state to my dates that I was not willing to make a commitment unless I was one hundred percent sure that I had found 'the one.' It was a disclaimer that if we were to be intimate, it wouldn't necessarily lead to a relationship. I didn't want to hurt anybody that I may date and wanted to make sure that we were on the same page. I also wanted to date a person who was secure and didn't need my affection in order to validate their self-worth and so this was an excellent test.

If you are having trouble keeping your heart open and if you are feeling hurt by the actions of your past lovers, then think about it like this; you only want to be with one person, don't you? If a person leaves you, forgive them. They are making the call that you were too afraid to make. They are making room in your life for you to have the relationship that you deserve. Let them go. Let your heart open and soften. If a person has left you, then you are one 'failed' relationship closer to finding the love of your life.

There is another key issue here that mostly affects women but others may still benefit from considering this. Typically, a woman is not allowed to be promiscuous in many cultures. I was single for a very long time and according to the rules of my society, I was not allowed to be sexually promiscuous.

For a long while, however, I craved intimacy. I had to seek intimacy under the guise of looking for 'the one.' At some point, I had to acknowledge that perhaps I was looking for love in all the wrong places because I was not *actually* looking for love. It turns out that I was only looking for an enjoyable intimate connection and I was not comfortable with this desire because of my past conditioning. By dating men who 'only wanted one thing,' I was able to shamelessly enjoy intimacy and then unwittingly place the blame on these men when they moved on, effectively using them as scapegoats.

Have you ever asked yourself, 'Why can't I be attracted to the nice guys?' or 'Why do I always go for the 'bad boy' types?' I took it as a positive sign I was ready to meet 'the one' when I finally started finding the nice guys attractive. This was a major milestone for me. It was the moment I finally knew that I was ready to make a commitment.

This may be a good time to reflect on your innermost intentions at the time of a heartbreak. What if you weren't completely ready to meet the love of your life? What if it was just nice to have some company? There is nothing wrong with wanting company or intimacy. Please note that I am not excusing any poor behaviour on the part of another; I am simply asking you to consider your role, especially if there is a pattern at play.

If you discover that you are just enjoying yourself and not yet ready for 'the one,' it is a good idea to either embrace this behaviour and fully accept it or change the behaviour. But either way, it is harmful to you to remain negatively attached to a person who may have hurt you in the past. Blaming others will only keep you stuck in old patterns.

If I had my time of being single over again, knowing what I know now, I would embrace the whole dating experience and revel in it, which, incidentally, is exactly the attitude I had before the man of my dreams walked into my life.

This is where faith and trust come in. When you believe and know that your perfect partner is on the way to you, then you will feel complete, you will be confident, sure of yourself, in love with life and you will be able to safely and surely navigate your way through the dating world, enjoying all of the stops along the way.

The purpose of dating is to learn who you are, to find out what you like and don't like and also to discover how magnetic and loveable you are! You are the one who calls the shots! If you are having a healthy dating life, then you won't expect every person you meet to fall madly and deeply in love with you. How can they? You are looking for that one special someone, aren't you? So why would everybody fall in love with you? This would be very counterproductive and potentially make choosing one partner very difficult.

If you are dating and haven't yet found 'the one,' then don't allow yourself to be hung up on the ones who didn't love you. They aren't for you. You want your ideal partner to love you for the truth of who you are, who you have been and who you are becoming.

If you experience setbacks in your love life, you need to trust the old cliché that this is for a reason. It is! It didn't work out because, for whatever reason, you and the other party did not see eye to eye. Bless these experiences and don't waste your time barking up the wrong tree.

If you are trying hard to make it work with the wrong person, or chasing the wrong types, then you're not free to allow your ideal person to come into your experience. I've seen so many people (myself included) become jaded when it doesn't work out with one person after the next.

Do your best to refrain from developing beliefs that create separation and anger towards the opposite sex (or preferred gender/energy polarity) such as 'all men are only interested in getting into my pants' or 'all women are neurotic.' It isn't true that all men are only interested in sex. But if you believe this, you will find evidence in your experience to support it.

It is possible that a particular man is only interested in you for sex because he knows in his heart that you are not the one for him but he finds you extremely alluring and believes you to be emotionally robust and mature enough to entertain a sexual relationship with you. This is a compliment, really it is. If it isn't how you roll, then don't go there. Learn to be discerning. Listen to your heart; it will guide you, which is precisely why you must keep your heart open.

Likewise, all women are not neurotic. If a man helps a woman to feel safe and extends a little generosity of spirit in reassuring her regularly, (and yes, probably for the entirety of the relationship) then she will not behave in a neurotic manner. All that is required is openness and honesty. Tell her truthfully what it is that you want. If you are looking for 'the one' and you are not prepared to make a commitment to her unless you are one hundred percent sure, then tell her this. She may still be hurt if you decide to end things but at least you have laid your cards on the table at the outset and it won't be as much of a shock. Once you've laid your cards on the table, she may still choose to be intimately involved with you or not but at least you have been transparent about where you both stand.

It is essential that you keep your heart open, even if it has not worked out in the past. You must see the past for the many blessings it has offered you and let go of any negative attachment to the relationships that did not work out or else you will bring all of this into your present and future relationships. An open heart is a heart that knows it is safe, that is filled with love and is sure that this love is powerful enough to transcend the greatest of heartaches.

Be honest now and take a moment to reflect on your past relationships. Don't dwell on them. Just take note and see if anything pops into your mind as being painful or unresolved.

Write a list of at least five things that you have gained from these relationships. Perhaps you have learned what it is that you want, such as, you want it to be easy and harmonious with your next lover. Perhaps you want to be true to yourself in your next relationship. Maybe you want to be able to trust your next partner and feel heard and validated when you speak to them. Perhaps you would like to have more things in common or be heading in a similar direction in life. Perhaps the past relationship was a complete disaster and you have learned that it is important to value yourself and not settle for less than you deserve.

Make a list now of whatever you have gained from your past relationship/s. You will know when you are ready to move on and when you have completely forgiven the past, by how you feel. In just a moment, I want you to think about your past relationship, close your eyes and go within to notice if there is any tension or tightness, perhaps in your abdomen, chest, jaw or throat. If there is tension or tightness, then perhaps you have not yet resolved or released the hurt from this relationship. And that's okay. Intend that this will dissolve for you in time.

If you are having trouble finding the positives of your past relationship, then it may be enough just to know that you don't want to have this experience again. Knowing what you don't want, will help you know exactly what it is that you do want. In this instance, it is best to just let go and focus on other things that make you feel good and make your heart soar with joy.

Simply know that the ideal person for you will be drawn to you when you are feeling at your absolute best, so focus on this instead. Keep your heart open and know that not all people are the same. You can attract something different next time.

If you are having recurrent negative experiences that seem to be of a similar nature, this is suggesting that there is a negative belief at play. If a negative pattern regularly emerges, then the recognition of the pattern, without judgement, will be enough to move you along in leaps and bounds. Simply allow yourself to soften. Be gentle and kind towards yourself. Just be aware of it as often as you can and soften each time that it becomes apparent to you. It will heal in time.

Timing is everything in this matter and when you finally do meet your lover, you will just know. You will be so happy and appreciative that they came to you precisely when they did. You will know with all of your heart that they came to you at just the right time. When my partner finally arrived after sixteen years of dating the 'wrong' guy, I was so happy that he came into my life exactly when he did. I finally understood why the Universe had kept me waiting for so long and I wished I hadn't wasted so many years fretting over his absence. His arrival in my life was inevitable! If only I had believed this! I would have played my cards differently.

I probably would have met and dated the exact same people at the exact same time, only I would have done it differently. I would have been more present. I would have embraced each moment with reverence and appreciation. I would have erred on the side of love rather than on the side of caution. I would have felt radiant and blissful and taken the absolute best care of myself. I would have done things that made me feel amazing and joyful and I would not have wasted my time on negative and self-destructive thoughts.

This is how it was for me in the moments leading up to meeting the man of my dreams. I became more balanced than ever. I started feeling in love, blissful and joyful. I met and magnetised some amazing and gorgeous men who were almost everything I had ever wished for. I enjoyed being with them but allowed great freedom. I knew on some level that there was something not entirely aligned with each man that I met and so I remained open because I just hadn't met 'the one' yet. Consequently, these people were wise, mature, stable, attractive and an absolute pleasure to be with! I felt as though my soul mate was already in my life because I was continuously magnetising new, amazing people into my life. And after glowing with love for two weeks, he was there, magnetised into my life, so swiftly and easily.

I was finally in the right place at the right time and I just knew that this was him. I recognised that he was coming because of other extraordinary men asking me out. I blessed and thanked the signs that the man of my dreams was, in fact, on his way to me. I didn't cling to any of the men, who were effectively signposts because I refused to compromise. I followed the easiest, most blissful-feeling path and energy and soon enough, with surprising ease, he became a part of my life.

Keep Your Heart Open

So, apparently, I can't say it enough! Keep your heart open! If you are magnetising partners into your life, who are almost (but not quite) everything you've ever hoped for, then it is a fabulous sign! Having any romantic interaction at all is a blessing! It is a signal of your ability to create the life of your dreams. It is showing you what you do or do not want. It is helping you to learn relationship skills and really home in on what is coming into your life. If you have hurts from the past, look again and see where your judgements may have created an image of that person that isn't really who they are.

It is extremely rare that anyone would intentionally hurt you. It may seem that way and they may let you believe it. If a person seems to have hurt you on purpose, it is much more likely that they were suffering or dysfunctional in some way already and you ended up being the one to get hurt, purely through interacting with them. You don't want these people in your life anyway, so if they are no longer in your life, then thank the Universe for showing you what you do not want and look forward to receiving something much better and brighter into your life.

Keep your heart open. It will magnetise a person to you who can take you to greater heights than you could have ever imagined possible. It will show you the way step by step. It will be your faithful guide now and ever more.

Chapter 4

Be the Person You Wish to Be

As an individual, you will grow and evolve in terms of who you are, what you enjoy doing and how you choose to function in the world. When I was eighteen years old and I dreamt of the man of my dreams, I so desperately wanted to meet him but at the same time, I am extremely happy I didn't meet him.

I didn't know it at the time but I was in the process of becoming a completely different person. Any man that I had attracted into my life would not have been the right person for me today, given who I was becoming. It is also more likely that had I met the man of my dreams, we probably wouldn't have noticed each other because I was not yet the person I have become today. I have undergone some major changes in my persona and lifestyle that made me more suitable for my ideal man.

Even though you are evolving as a human being and in a perpetual state of becoming, it can still be good to have an idea of who you wish to be in this world. From a much broader perspective, there is an essential part of you that will remain unchanged; a part that loves unconditionally and experiences the world unconditionally. But relationships must satisfy you on multiple levels.

You can fall in love with a person from a spiritual perspective but because you exist in a physical reality, your lifestyle and habits must also be a match. If you want to attract the right person into your life, it is imperative that you get to know yourself, really know yourself, at a deeper level.

The more genuine you can be about who you are, what you desire and what you really feel, the better you will be able to recognise whether you have made a sound decision about your future lover. If you feel that you have been attracting the 'wrong' types, then it might be worthwhile reflecting on how authentic you are being and how true to yourself you are.

Do you often attenuate your behaviours and go along with what others want just for the sake of having a person in your life? Would you rather spend time with people you don't really connect with just for the sake of having somebody around or are you happy to be alone? It can sometimes be scary to make changes that honour who you are, especially if you are frightened of ending up alone.

There was a time when I noticed some of my friends falling away because I was making new decisions that were more in keeping with who I felt I was becoming as a person. This was frightening for a short while because I felt lonely and wondered if I would ever meet like-minded people. But I conceded I was better off finding people who love me for who I really am.

When you find things you love doing and when you stay true to who you really are, you will find that wonderful, genuine people will walk into your life. You will enjoy each other's company because you have more in common due to shared mutual interests.

Become proactive about learning who you are and what you enjoy doing. If you don't have many hobbies or interests, then make a date with a friend (or even set a date with yourself) to try something new, even if it is only once a month.

You might not like the activity and that is fine because you are learning who you are and what you do and don't enjoy doing. By spending time with a friend, (or going out and meeting new people) you are also realising how loveable you are and you might discover new skills and talents that you didn't know you had.

When you imagine the person of your dreams, it might also help to ask yourself 'What kind of person would my ideal lover wish to date?' and 'Am I the person I wish to be in order to attract such a person?' It is important, however, not to change yourself into something that is not authentically who you are. The idea is to make sure that your outside matches your inside. Then you become the remarkable person that you know you can be.

If you want to be with somebody who is active and adventurous, for example and you're spending all of your time sitting on the lounge, eating potato chips and watching television, then it is unlikely that you're going to meet an active and adventurous person.

Please note that I didn't say it is *impossible* to meet such a person, however, it is *unlikely*, as you're not putting yourself in a position where it will be easy to cross paths with such a person.

This is basically what I was doing when I had a dream about my ideal partner! I was studying at the time and I was unfit, unhealthy and I didn't really go out much. I decided to spend more time outdoors and in nature because I wanted to meet people who enjoyed spending time outdoors and in nature.

You do not have to become the exact same person you want to date. It's just a good idea to be a person your ideal partner would want to date. Having some activities in common can be really helpful for coming together with another person harmoniously.

If you want to meet a person who is fit and healthy because you also want to be fit and healthy, then it is a great idea to become a person who is fit and healthy. Research ways to take excellent care of your health, how to eat well and ways to exercise that you might enjoy. Get proactive about improving your life in ways that you wish to, so that when your ideal person walks into your life, you are proud of who you are, you love who you are and you can't wait to openly and honestly share all that you are with them.

Being fit is just one example of something you might wish to achieve but remember, this isn't important to everyone. If this doesn't matter to you, then focus on what does matter. Perhaps you've always wanted to take a cooking class to become a fabulous cook and perhaps your ideal person loves and appreciates eating. Perhaps you've always fantasised about serenading your lover with a romantic song played on an acoustic guitar and your ideal partner has always fantasised about a lover who can play guitar.

Maybe you have been waiting for your partner to come into your life before you make these changes. If you have been holding off on changing because 'what's the point? I don't have anybody to cook for, sing for,' or whatever the case may be, then it is time to think again.

Go out into the world and get ready now. You will be doing yourself a massive favour, regardless of whether your partner walks into your life tomorrow or five years from now. Don't you want to be pleased with who you are? Don't you want to be living your best life; a life that you enjoy and can be proud of?

A side-effect of making these changes is that you will be putting a huge signal out to the Universe saying 'I am now pleased with who I am and I am ready to invite the most amazing person into my life.'

You will also be far more likely to put yourself in the right place at the right time in order to meet the love of your life and you may as well be having fun while you're 'waiting' for them to show up in your experience anyway, right?

Chapter 5

Discover Your Worth

There is a major side-effect of being raised in a society that seems to reward only effort and hard work, where you are expected to earn your keep and you are frowned upon if you are seen to be simply swanning your way through life. This is evidenced by sayings such as, 'Nothing worth having comes easy' and you're probably not even batting an eyelid at this right now; that's just how it is, right?

You have been inadvertently trained to believe that you do not deserve to receive anything good unless you put in the hard work or become a better person, become better looking, earn more money, have more to offer and the list goes on.

As you start to make positive changes in your thinking and beliefs, you will begin to realise something very significant that has always been and always will be; you are already worthy of all of the dreams in your heart, including meeting the love of your life.

It is only your current human society that tells you, 'You are not worthy.' This is a bogus belief that very much needs to change if you want to allow the things you desire to come into your experience.

While it is good to focus on becoming a person you are proud of, it is also essential to maintain a balance and remember that you are already enough. Be sure to remember that you already deserve people in your life who love you exactly as you are and are also happy for you as you make positive life changes.

You're improving yourself to become the person you wish to be for your own benefit. A consequence of focusing your attention on becoming that which you wish to be, is that you will naturally increase your appreciation of yourself and attract people into your life who also appreciate you.

It may not even be necessary to change all that much, as you may have already decided that you're satisfied with exactly how you are conducting your life in order to attract your perfect mate.

If this is where you're at, it will be helpful to take some time to acknowledge that you are already everything you wish to be and to state to yourself that the person who gets to be with you is the luckiest person alive. I mean it.

Say it right now; 'The person who gets to be with me is the luckiest person alive!'

Thank you for indulging me. Please note how it felt to say those words. If it felt good to say those words, this is an excellent sign. You can use this sentence to amplify your self-appreciation. If it didn't feel good, then something is shifting for you, which is also advantageous. You can use this sentence to help shift any false beliefs that are creating blockages in your energy.

If, on the other hand, there is much that you would like to change, then it is beneficial to find appreciation of exactly who you are, even during the process of making any changes. If you don't love who you are now and if you're averse to facing this, it will make creating lasting change more challenging.

Be kind and gentle and appreciate as much as you can about who you are, no matter how simple it is. It could be as simple as enjoying and being appreciative of the sense of warmth in your body. Perhaps you feel blessed to be able to sense the golden glow of the sun on your skin. Perhaps you appreciate your ability to perceive beauty in nature. Be sure to look for things that you can appreciate right now and make your self-improvements from a space of loving kindness.

It is not selfish or conceited to appreciate and revel in the 'self.' If you value yourself, then you are in a much better position to choose circumstances that are desirable. Find a place of gentle acceptance within you and make any desired changes from that space.

If you are trying to make changes through a sense of incompleteness, unworthiness and by berating yourself, it is possible that you are going to give up trying to make the change because it doesn't feel good.

The best way to create lasting and positive changes in your life, is to love yourself first. Acknowledge that you are already loveable. Acknowledge that you are already worthy. Look for where you are already succeeding. Then make the changes you wish to make; not because you loathe the way things are but because you love yourself enough to want something better, that is more in alignment with who you are becoming.

In order to be open to love and to magnetise your soul mate to you, it is ideal if you feel worthy, fulfilled, complete and that you love and appreciate all that you are. Starting new activities and spending time with friends who love you, is a terrific way to remember how loveable you are and how worthy you are of having love in your life.

If you enjoy writing, you may also like to get a notepad and write a list of things that you appreciate about your life. You can state these things aloud if you prefer. Expressing aloud that which you appreciate is a highly effective way to raise your vibration and to shift into a positive state.

Discover Your Worth

Feeling worthy might be as simple as acknowledging that you are a kind and caring person. Perhaps you have a fabulous sense of humour and a wit to be reckoned with. Perhaps you are playful and enjoy laughing. Perhaps you have a special talent. Maybe you are the type of person others feel safe around and can confide in.

See if you can come up with at least twenty things that you appreciate about yourself. And then state 'I am worthy of love because...' and follow on with the reasons you are worthy of love.

Your reasons might be as simple as 'I am worthy of love because I am a gentle person who exists on this planet and has a heart that is full of warmth and appreciation' or 'I am worthy of love because I am.' You really don't have to have any complicated or fancy reasons for why you are worthy, as you are already worthy simply by your existence.

This exercise serves as a reminder that you are a unique individual and you have much value to offer. There is somebody out there who loves your own brand of uniqueness and weirdness and totally 'gets you,' just as you are.

You are worthy. You were born worthy. Don't believe what you were taught by an unconscious society. Tell yourself every day of your worth. Write it down or say it aloud. You are worthy of everything your heart desires. You were born worthy. You deserve love. You deserve everything that is good.

Chapter 6

Don't Settle for Second Best

A worthy person; a person who knows their value (that's you), will not compromise on what it is that they wish for. One of the biggest issues I see for people involved in dissatisfying long-term relationships, is that they have 'settled' for a relationship that was not ideal for them.

I often hear people say that there were 'red flags' in the beginning that they chose to ignore. Why? Sometimes it is because there is chemistry in the beginning. I know of many people who have ignored signs that their partner was not right for them because they had powerful feelings of chemistry and connection.

As you spend time with a person and as you get to know them better, you will become more familiar with that person's energy and it will begin to feel quite natural to you. The contrast in energy that was experienced as a 'spark' will become more natural and will soften. This is known as the honeymoon effect and it will fade in time.

When you are with the right person, you will still have a deep and lasting connection that is beyond the initial euphoria of the honeymoon period. But if you are with somebody purely because of chemistry and you have ignored initial signs that you are not compatible with one another, it will most likely lead to a very unhappy association.

If you settle for less than you deserve, both of you will end up unhappy within your relationship. If you cannot accept a person as they are, then you deserve to be with somebody who is what you wish for and they deserve to be with somebody who loves them, just as they are.

You don't do anyone any favours by compromising. What will happen when you decide to make a major commitment with one another such as buying a house together or having children? Do you want to have children who have the characteristics of your partner? Is this a person you can see yourself being happy with in the long-term? These questions might be worth considering if you want something truly magnificent and not just something that is 'safe.'

The reality is that there is no such thing as a relationship or life situation that is safe. All forms on this earth are subject to change and it will be wise to keep this in mind, as you move through your journey of life, for the purpose of embracing your moments.

I know of a person who settled for less than she wanted because she believed she could change her partner. She could see his potential and the amazing man that he could one day be. After years of being together with him, she assured me, 'He will be a better partner once we are married.' But the dynamic in the relationship did not change for the better. In fact, after the wedding, the relationship was exactly the same and he did not change his behaviour at all. It became apparent that this man's 'actual' did not match his 'potential.'

It is not your job to change another person. That person has to want to change. If you are trying to change someone; if there are essential things about a person you do not like, irrespective of their potential, then chances are that this person is not for you. This book isn't about finding a project to rescue or to mould into your perfect person. This book is about knowing how to recognise your perfect person and prepare yourself for their arrival.

Another reason that you may be tempted to settle for something less than your ideal, is because of a scarcity belief. If you have ever caught yourself saying something along the lines of 'All the good ones are taken' or 'I'm running out of time,' you have been falling victim to scarcity beliefs.

If a scarcity belief is active in your energy, it is likely to colour your view of the world and will therefore be reflected in your life experience. If you believe that all of the good ones are married, for example, then you will start noticing a lot of desirable married people.

If you have a scarcity belief, there may be the temptation to cling to a person because you believe that they are a 'safe' bet. Since all forms in life, including relationships, are subject to change, the concept of 'safe' is redundant. Is the illusion of safety something that you are willing to trade your happiness for?

I know it can be scary to go out on a limb in the hope of finding some seemingly lofty ideal but what would you rather? Would you rather be in an ultimately unfulfilling relationship or would you like to create an opportunity for something genuinely special?

There is nothing wrong with having an interim partner or a relationship that doesn't work out. With each person you get to know, you learn. You learn about yourself. You learn about your preferences. You learn how to communicate within a relationship, how to develop trust, cooperation and so on.

There are so many people who have said, 'The signs were there; I ignored them and now look at the mess I'm in.' That 'mess' being children involved, years of emotional abuse and a nasty and difficult divorce, just to give a real-life example.

But even a so-called 'mess' isn't the end of the world. So much beauty can be gained from such a situation and those children are such a blessing! Those children are an exclusive blend of two people and exist exactly in the form that they exist in because of the two people who created them. Even if the relationship has ended, something truly splendid has arisen.

But those of you who haven't encountered this situation may have an opportunity to choose differently. Of course, you must honour your heart and do what feels right to you. I really mean that. I cannot possibly know you or your life situation as I write this. But if you do wish for something extraordinary, then being involved with something ordinary, probably won't lead you to the life of your dreams. Learn what it is that you want and once you do, date only extraordinary people. You deserve the best. It is time to stop selling yourself short.

Chapter 7

Find Completeness Within

Achieving a sense of completeness within, on a consistent basis, is absolutely essential if you wish to be in a healthy relationship. There are so many people who are looking for a lover to complete them.

Many children learn that when they make their suffering obvious and loud enough, that is, throwing a tantrum; caregivers who desperately seek relief from the commotion will give them what they want. And some children unwittingly carry this lesson through to adulthood.

The nature of the Universe, however, is not to reward detrimental behaviour in the same way that some caregivers do. As a result, some of you may feel that you are suffering without your other half and cannot be happy until they are in your life. If you are suffering and feeling incomplete without your other half, then you are choosing to live your life in a conditional way. Living life conditionally means that you only offer your love and acceptance of life based on whether or not conditions are satisfactory to you. This can result in falling victim to your circumstances and your happiness can become dependent on factors that are out of your control.

If this is the case, you will be likely to attract other people who are also feeling incomplete and will make you the source of their happiness. You may also find yourself ignoring vital warning signs and red flags that a person will not be the best match for you because of your need to have a partner in order to initially alleviate that suffering. A relationship where you are each dependent on the other for your happiness will often lead to emotional manipulation and resentment.

Please keep in mind, however, that a relationship that happens out of this space is not necessarily a failure or a mistake. It is okay to take a detour on your way to the love of your life. You will find that you will learn about how to be in a relationship and learn about your preferences. If you experience a relationship that appears to have failed and if you have ignored the warning signs in the past, it is okay. Acknowledge all that your past relationship has given you and resolve to choose differently next time. Resolve to find a better feeling place when you next allow a lover into your life.

When you are feeling complete within, you will not *need* another person in your life. It will just be a delightful bonus! When you are feeling incomplete, there will be a neediness and desperation in you that is almost palpable and repellent to the people who can offer you an enjoyable and fulfilling relationship.

Feeling complete does not have to take a long time. If you can bring your attention into the present moment and place your awareness acutely within your physical body, you may notice a deep sense of peace and belonging that is always present within you. It sounds very simple and it is but it does require some practice.

Meditation is an excellent tool for bringing your awareness into the present moment and into the physical body. As you pay attention to your breathing, as you connect with your body and with who you really are at a deeper level, you will feel your oneness; your completeness, that is always available to you, in the here and now.

Any state that you practice repeatedly will eventually become a predominant state in your experience. If you meditate on being present, even just for fifteen minutes a day, that sense of peace and completeness will infiltrate your experience. If you can feel complete on your own and feel happy in your own company, it will make your dating journey much more enjoyable and harmonious.

You've probably noticed that the habit of complaining is difficult to break and this is because we tend to practice it often but the good news is, the more you practice feeling good, the better you will feel and this will begin taking over your experience. It will be easier for you to feel good, to feel complete and to feel peaceful when you practice being present for a short while each day.

Finding The One

I was single for a long time before I met my ideal partner. I had the premonition about him when I was eighteen years old and met him when I was thirty-four years old. He is eleven years younger than I am. When I had my dream, I just knew he was coming. I just knew he would find me and I just knew it would be at exactly the right time.

My biggest regret in my dating life was that I didn't revel in being single for longer. Once you have found your partner, that is it. You will never be alone, ever again. Enjoy your time alone! Make the most of it. I wish I hadn't spent so much of my single life searching for and fretting over whether each person I was dating was the boy from my dream. What a waste of invaluable experiences! Ideally, I would have been present, felt complete and allowed my life to flow naturally, without trying to force things.

About two weeks before I met my soul mate, I decided I was going to feel good, no matter what. I decided I was going to feel as if he was already in my life. I meditated every morning and every night. My meditations focused on feeling in love, on my heart expanding and on magnetising love into my life.

And the most extraordinary experiences began happening. I started seeing things and people that I loved everywhere! I started having more experiences of love in my daily life and I was absolutely glowing! I felt so complete, that I was no longer concerned whether I met him or not!

Find Completeness Within

And then within two weeks of meditating in this way, our paths finally crossed and it was magical.

There was no question that we were perfect for each other. If only I had spent the prior sixteen years believing that my life was worthy. If only I had given my absolute love and acceptance to my various life situations during my singledom. And if I could set an intention for you, it would be that you can find completeness within, prior to any manifestation. I would intend that you can appreciate your single life and fall in love with everything that is presently in your experience, with or without your soul mate. Which leads us to the next chapter.

Chapter 8

Fall in Love with Life

It is vital that you aren't expecting a partner to make you happy, to alleviate your suffering or to rectify a sense of feeling incomplete. Needing another person to complete you from a state of lack or desperately wanting anything in your life, is an admission to the Universe that you do not already have it.

If you feel incomplete and if you are feeling as though life is intolerable without having romance to complete you, then you are setting a tone that will block your progress with finding your ideal companion. This does not mean that you won't find a partner (although it will be less likely). It does mean that you are more likely to attract a partner who is detrimental to your well-being in some way or that you will extract the worst out of one another.

It is critical to be brave here and ask yourself truthfully if you are feeling as though you are suffering without a partner and if you believe your life will be better for having them. If you are already in love with life, in love with yourself and feeling complete exactly as you are, then you are on the right path towards allowing the love of your life to enter your experience.

If you want to attract the perfect relationship to you and allow your romantic relationship to soar to greater and greater heights of love, then it is essential that you learn to fall in love with life, regardless of whether you have met the partner of your dreams.

When you fall in love with life, you will bring a person into your life naturally and easily, who will simply mirror back to you the joy and love that you have found independently of one another. This can and will enhance your life exponentially.

How do you fall in love with life? Practice unconditional happiness, acceptance and love. This means that you fall in love simply because you exist. It is a state that can take a little bit of practice, depending on your natural disposition.

I was raised in a very painful and violent household. For a long time, I associated love with pain and I equated life with suffering. Consequently, falling in love with my existence would have been an absurd concept at one stage. But now, falling in love with my own existence is a surprising reality.

The practice of unconditional acceptance is groundbreaking, in that, once you get good at it, you can find a sense of relief, anywhere, anytime and irrespective of your circumstances.

You can allow the world to be, allow others to be, allow things to come and go and you can love and appreciate it all. It requires nothing; you don't expect anything and yet, when you enter this state, things work out for you. This is because you begin to notice when things are working out, having found a new and more positive perspective.

Unconditional happiness is found when you fully enter and accept your present moment reality. It is found when you stop trying and start allowing. It is found when you release your inner tension and complaints about how things are and simply observe without judgement or negativity.

You will know when you have found unconditional happiness, as you will notice a subtle feeling of peace and stillness. This feeling is always available to you when you make a decision to relinquish any attachment to negativity. This feeling can grow and become much stronger and more palpable as you practice it.

There are some excellent tools, such as affirmations, meditation and practicing presence, that can help you to enter a state of unconditional acceptance and happiness. I will address each of these in detail in later chapters.

Another really simple way of falling in love with life, is to make a point of noticing the conditions in your life that please you. If you take fifteen minutes every day to think about or write down the things in your life that you appreciate, you will begin to fall in love with your life. This will place you in an excellent position to allow the most magnificent people to find you.

The conditions that are in your life that please you won't necessarily be the same as the things that please me but I will do my best to offer some general examples here of things that you may like to notice and appreciate.

Let's just say that you are completely miserable and you're thinking, 'what on earth could I possibly have to feel good about?' Then it is probably a good idea to start with some very basic things. Can you take your attention to your breathing now? Can you feel a gentle movement in your chest and abdomen? Can you notice a gentle pulse throughout your entire body? Go ahead, take some time now and bring your attention to your body.

Marvel at how air is taken into your lungs, how oxygenated blood is circulated through your body via your heart, gently, silently pulsing and moving life-giving oxygen throughout your entire body and removing and cleansing all that is no longer needed. Take some time to appreciate this silent servant that continues on, even in your sleep, caring for you, tending to your needs.

Does your body serve you well? Can you move from place to place? Can you eat and taste food that you love? Do you enjoy being hungry and then eating the most fabulous tasting food? Do you enjoy the feeling of the sun on your skin or breathing fresh air? What about the scent of a flower in bloom? Can you see and appreciate a gorgeous sunset or smell the fresh rain on the wet earth? Do you enjoy taking a walk on the beach, breathing in the salt air, feeling the refreshing breeze against your skin and the sand beneath your feet? Do you have a pet that you adore, who loves you unconditionally?

As you can see, you don't need to have extraordinary, big things in your life in order to be pleased about your situation. You can find satisfaction by acknowledging the small and simple things that please you. This exercise is simply about finding and appreciating the things in your life that bring a sense of peace, joy and contentment.

For fifteen minutes each day, look for the things that you love and do your best to stay off any topics that concern you. Take fifteen minutes every day to dedicate to feeling good (more if you like). Finding things to love and falling in love with your life will go a very long way towards attracting the life of your dreams.

But don't fall into the trap of using these techniques purely for the purpose of finding a partner. Use these techniques because it feels good to use them. Use them because regardless of whether the perfect partner walks into your life tomorrow or ten years from now, you have won already.

You have won already because you have fallen in love with life and you feel complete. You already have the life of your dreams and if somebody comes into your life, they are going to have to be extraordinary because you will not settle for second best; your life is amazing right now and nobody else could ever add anything to your life that you don't already have!

When this person comes into your life, when you are in this blissful state, you will know that they are perfect for you, as they will be magnetised to you at just the right time, when you have already found the secret, the magic and the true perfection of life.

Chapter 9

Let Go and Trust

I know that to let go and to trust is easier said than done. Let's say you're holding onto an object with your hand. It seems simple to 'let go' of it, right? But what if you're not even aware that you're holding onto something? We've all had those moments when we've been holding our car keys and have frantically searched the house, unable to find them. Oh, you haven't done that? What about looking for your sunglasses when they've been on top of your head the whole time?

What if you're so used to holding on to anxiety, for example, that it has become your natural state and you don't even know how it feels to be otherwise? The anxiety is there but you're no longer aware of it.

It's just like the nose on your face. You can see it all the time but because it's always there, it serves you to ignore it and so it barely enters your awareness, unless you notice something on it that isn't normally there, like a pimple.

Subconscious beliefs are a little like this. You tune them out as a way of functioning. And you will be able to function quite normally most of the time, unless there is some kind of flareup. But you don't need to grab your torch and pitchfork to hunt down anything that does not serve you.

Once you have begun a journey of self-exploration, awareness and spiritual growth, any belief or state of being that may be hindering your progress will become apparent. It will become uncomfortable to be in a state that is out of alignment with your inner truth or to hold negative beliefs and you will need to face them calmly, with presence and awareness.

If there is anything that is standing in the way of your desires, you don't need to dig around and find them. Don't worry about looking for whatever it is that may be holding your desire apart from you. Life will bring these things to the forefront of your awareness and at precisely the right time.

Your primary task in magnetising your soul mate to you is to find a feeling of love and peace within and to broadcast this feeling or *vibration*. This is the very energy that will draw exactly the right people and circumstances into your life.

Letting go and trusting in something that is unseen is not always easy for us physically focussed, materially oriented mere mortals. There may be times when you will question the validity of your desire. There may be times when you have been doing your part and feeling good, only to find that situations and circumstances appear to be working against you. It can be very confusing. But all is not as it seems.

If you have been asking for what you believe to be 'big' and 'fantastic' dreams to come true, then you are likely going to be challenging any rigid beliefs you may hold in opposition to your desire. You will need to acknowledge these beliefs eventually, so if things appear to be going 'wrong,' perhaps it is time to look a little closer.

This is especially true if you have been taking positive steps to feel good, to feel love and to feel bliss. What comes to you is always for your benefit. There is always an opportunity hidden within any potential 'disaster' and often you won't see what this hidden gem is until hindsight comes into play.

If things appear to be going wrong, if it becomes difficult to trust and you've had enough of the manifestation movement, it is a good time to use some self-coaching. You may like to use an affirmation such as 'Something good will come of this. I don't know what it is right now. But I will know in time. Something good will come of this. Something good will come of this.'

If you are losing your ability to let go and trust, then consider this; what if it doesn't work? What if all of this manifestation stuff is just a lie and feeling good and blissful won't bring you the things you want or the partner of your dreams? Do you then want to feel bad instead? Is feeling good such a terrible price to pay?

If techniques for manifestation don't bring your manifestation to fruition and you consider them to be ineffective, then perhaps you might decide to do what it takes to feel good and in love for the sake of feeling good and in love.

This is what letting go and trusting is. It is knowing that ultimately, the only thing you want is to feel good, even if you can't see the things that you wish for yet. In the two weeks before I finally met my soul mate, I was fed up with suffering. I was fed up with being hung up on men that weren't available to me and didn't love me. I was fed up with feeling like I was chasing guys all the time.

I finally decided that feeling good was the most important thing. I made a commitment to do whatever was necessary, in order to feel good. I decided to fall in love with life and live as though my soul mate was with me already.

To my surprise, when I had achieved this state of being in love, it didn't matter that he wasn't with me! I was no longer concerned if my lover was in my experience or not. I was simply revelling in life! Soul mate or no soul mate, I was happy, content, pleased, blissed-out, joyous, excited, free and enjoying my life experience.

Letting go and trusting is being brave enough to be happy for no particular reason. Finding a way to relax and enjoy your life experience, is letting go. Not reading too deeply into anything unwanted and simply observing calmly, is trusting. Allowing your life experiences to come and go freely, without judging or analysing, is trusting.

Meditation is a big help in learning to achieve a state of trust. When you connect with yourself inwardly, it becomes easier to know your worth, to sense your completeness and to feel that you are loved and secure.

By bringing your awareness into the moment, your mind cannot project into the future and worry about things going wrong. When you become good at practicing this state of presence and quieting your mind, you will find that this state will carry over into your experience of life more often.

Any negative belief patterns, judgments, complaints or other reactive mental patterns and habits are practiced states of mind. You will have noticed that if you have tried to stop being angry, for example, it is difficult to do so because it is a habit that you have developed and practiced.

There is no need to worry about negative states or anything that you wish to eradicate. As you practice meditation and positive states, these will gradually become your new, practiced states. You will still have an entire range of emotions but you will be able to access the state of presence more easily and so, you will find relief in each moment. You will give yourself respite from negativity more easily. And in this moment, you will find sanctuary, you will find trust and you will know that all is well. You will not be concerned about the future or the unfoldment of your dreams because you will be happy to reside in the here and now.

From this space, as a delightful side-effect, miraculous things can flow to you and if they don't, it doesn't matter because you are too busy enjoying your happiness. You have let go and you have learned to trust because you know your innate well-being, you know your worth, you feel loved and adored and that is enough.

Chapter 10

How to Let Go and Trust

It's easy to say 'let go and trust.' It is easy to explain how to let go and how to trust. But carrying out the letting go and trusting may require practice, self-reflection and dedication. In my case, developing the ability to trust required constant self-coaching and self-awareness.

I began coaching myself at a very young age in order to make it through some difficult times. There was a gentle voice of reason within me that made some excellent and valid points when it came to trusting. I eventually conceded that it is vital to trust yourself and to trust in life. I also discovered that there is a big difference between being trusting and being discerning. I will address this shortly.

In my teenage years, I had difficulty trusting my peers and it wasn't without reason. I had been very naïve and I was shattered to realise that my so-called friends could commit some horrible acts of betrayal. Well, that is how it seemed at the time. These days, I couldn't care less! All of your problems seem so much bigger in your teen years.

I was lost, confused and suffering a significant amount of emotional upheaval. I was also very paranoid about being betrayed again. But I had a gentle voice in my head that said to me, 'Even if your ex-friend is spreading rumours about you, what do you plan to do about it? Do you wish to confront this person? Do you wish to retaliate? How do you see it playing out? Are you prepared to act on it?'

The answer was that none of the available options were appealing to me. Whether or not my ex-friend had betrayed me made absolutely no difference to our relationship; we were no longer friends. Therefore, there was nothing I wished to do in response to my fears. I couldn't censor this person and stop them from saying nasty things about me, nor could I know with absolute certainty that they were saying anything nasty at all. There was no action I could take to control my ex-friend or anyone else. So, there was only one viable choice that I had remaining. I had to let it go. And I had to coach myself through the process.

Every time I felt myself becoming fearful or hurt, I simply had to tell myself, 'There is nothing that you can do. It is best to put it out of your mind. Remain in this moment. Keep your attention on what is immediately before you and stop trying to predict what may or may not happen in the future.'

I was trying to protect myself from being hurt in the future but this was not possible. We can only ever cope with what is presented to us at any given point in time. Being fearful of what may happen in the future will only squander what you have right here and now.

There was a significant lesson in all of this. I learned that my former friend was not the kind of person I could divulge secrets to and it was best not to share intimate details with them if I wanted those details to remain private and if I did not want to be mocked or judged.

This is the difference between being discerning and trusting. There was no need to be fearful. It was simply a matter of making a choice. Am I prepared to share sensitive information with this person or not? That is all.

It is essential to learn to trust when you are dating. Being discerning is also important but this is more about trusting yourself and your own judgement. You will know in time how to trust yourself and it is okay to get it wrong sometimes. This is how we learn. And in your discovery of people and of yourself, you get to choose how much of yourself you wish to give and how much you would like to be involved with a person.

When I was in my early twenties, I met a really attractive young man. We had great chemistry but to be honest, I wasn't really sure what I was looking for at the time. It was just nice getting to know this gorgeous young man who made my heart beat so fast every time he was near. It became apparent that I was becoming addicted to the delectable flood of endorphins I experienced in his company. We were officially dating but we weren't physically intimate. I was looking for something long-term and wanted to be sure of him before giving away the goods. I wasn't prepared to share that much of myself with him if it turned out to be just a fling.

Our time together was fun but he kept talking about this girl he knew, a lot! One day, I pointed this out to him. I said, 'You're talking about... let's call her Cynthia... a lot. Is there something going on romantically with Cynthia? Do you like her?' He told me that there was nothing going on with Cynthia, that she was just a friend and he was with me, so there was no need to be concerned.

Now, the way that I saw it was that I had one of two choices; I could continue to worry and be paranoid until I finally pushed him away and ruined what could have led to a fun and fulfilling long-term relationship or I could put Cynthia out of my mind, trust what he said to me, just continue to enjoy being in a relationship with him and see where it led.

I decided to just let it go. I had to be present, intensely present. I had to remain in the moment and spend my time with him, just being with him. Our time together was enjoyable.

But then one evening, he was very distant and he told me he wanted to break up. I asked him, 'Is there somebody else?' with the subtext being 'Is this because of Cynthia?' He paused and I saw his eyes look up and to the left.

Strangely, at that very moment, I had an image in my mind of him kissing Cynthia. To this day, I have never let him know of the insight I had in that moment. I suspected immediately that it was because of her that he was breaking up with me.

The strange thing is, it actually would have made me feel better if he had been sincere with me. You see, I sensed that he really liked her from our earlier conversations and I didn't want to be someone's second best. I suppose he just didn't realise that the girl of his dreams was excited by him also and so, he was 'settling' for me.

I didn't want to be with somebody who wasn't excited to be with me. I really liked him but I wanted the feeling to be mutual. My suspicion was confirmed when he turned up at a social gathering a week later, hand-in-hand with Cynthia. I wasn't devastated. The signs had always been there. I was pleased for him, even though it was a little bit awkward. I had a great sense of accomplishment at how I had conducted myself within the relationship.

The outcome would have been exactly the same, regardless of my behaviour. Either way, he was going to end up with Cynthia. But this way, I got to love with an open heart, I got to hold my head high, I got to let go, I got to learn how to trust and now I get to share this story with you. Even to this day, I am happy that he found her. I am pleased that I parted ways with him lovingly. It has all worked out perfectly.

On the other hand, I could have made things very troublesome between us. I could have claimed ownership of him. I could have harassed him for constant reassurance. I could have become fearful, angry and ugly. But why? To what end? In the end, there is nothing to forgive. He has done nothing wrong. Even if he did, in fact, cheat on me, it was the 'right' thing because I was not the one for him. I wanted to be with the man of my dreams and a man who loves somebody else is clearly not the man of my dreams, is he?

Trust is essential in a relationship. If somebody doesn't want to be with you, there is absolutely nothing you can do. Life will happen. You will not live happily ever after. This is a myth simply because you cannot live forever. Your relationship will always be temporary, as will everything in life. This is not negativity; this is simply stating the truth of the impermanence of all physical things.

That is why it is important to learn to let go, to trust life and trust the people in your life. If you have done your best to find out who a person is (and your best is all that you can do) and you have decided to spend time with that person and share all that you are with them, then you have no choice but to embrace and enjoy each precious moment you share. Being intensely present is the key. Each moment, every relationship, every construct in your life will come to pass one day. Don't trade out your moments now because you are too busy worrying about an imagined future.

Chapter 11

Practice Appreciation

Practicing appreciation is far more powerful than I can ever express in words. But before we address the practice of appreciation, I would like to make sure you're aware that you want everything you want because you believe that the having of that thing will make you happy. Well, yes, having things can make you happy. But you can also be happy when you have very little.

Alternatively, having things can make you unhappy. This is because sometimes, once you have possession of something, there may be a tendency to worry about losing it or to become concerned about protecting it. A brand-new car is a perfect example. I'm sure you've seen it before, when a shiny and expensive vehicle is acquired and the owner will then proceed to panic every time somebody comes close to it. They obsess over it and have to park it only in certain places or only next to other shiny and new cars. If a friend looks as though they may spill something on the brand-new leather seats, the owner of the vehicle will appear to be anything but emotionally balanced. Depending on the owner of the vehicle, it may appear that the acquisition of this dream car is more of a burden and source of stress than a source of joy.

This is where becoming established in your happiness, prior to acquiring your dreams, can be really helpful. And yes, you can be happy prior to receiving the relationship of your dreams. Do you really want to meet somebody when you are feeling miserable or incomplete? Do you want to place all of your hopes, dreams and expectations upon them, only to realise that they are going to die one day or maybe fall out of love with you and leave you, then spend the rest of your time together worrying about if (or when) the aforementioned might happen?

But if you can be in love with life and happy alone, if you can celebrate your days as they evolve and be excited to expand in your love no matter what, you can allow that relationship to enter your life and you will not let fear hinder your ability to love.

Being in a relationship is a constant balancing act between being your own source of love and receiving the love of your partner. It is a constant adjustment of your ability to love yourself and not depend on your partner as the source of your happiness.

Your partner will never be the source of your love and appreciation. You are the one who allows or disallows your innate wellbeing. You are the one who makes the decision to allow yourself to be open to the flow of loving energy from your Source. When you choose to fully embrace a given life situation, you allow this powerful flow of love. When you offer inner resistance to a situation, you deny yourself this powerful flow of loving energy. Your partner can mirror this love back to you and can be somebody with whom you can create more love, expansion and joy and with whom you can celebrate this ever-expanding joyous state. But it is beneficial to remember that they are never your *source* of love. Making somebody your source of love is placing an impossible expectation upon them, which no human can fulfill and which will lead to a negative undertone within the relationship.

Why is appreciation so powerful? Appreciation is extremely magnetic. Have you ever noticed how favourably you behave towards somebody who offers thanks to you? When you are appreciative, you will draw favourable people and circumstances to you. Appreciation not only achieves phenomenal results but it causes you to feel incredible right now. Appreciation gives you a sense of completeness. Appreciation helps you to feel connected with your inner power and as though a benevolent force is taking care of you. Appreciation helps you feel love and feel loved. Appreciation will allow your heart to sing and expand your sense of joy. When you are appreciative, you feel as though you already have everything and that nothing in the world could ever add to what you already have. When you are appreciative, you don't need a lover in your life because you are already in love. And when you don't need anything, you allow everything. When you allow everything to be exactly as it is, you love without condition.

Have you ever noticed how those who love without condition, without expectation, naturally magnetise you to them? You feel safe and you know you can be yourself and not tread on eggshells because you are certain that you cannot make this person unhappy without due cause. They are happy anyway. They are reasonable and understanding. Even if you accidentally say or do the wrong thing, it doesn't matter; they are still ultimately secure. It feels nice to be around these people because you can relax and be at ease.

A person such as this will still have preferences about how to behave but they will communicate clearly, for they are not afraid to be true to themselves and therefore you can feel safe to be yourself.

Practicing appreciation, funnily enough, requires practice. It really does. There is so much negative self-talk that is culturally conditioned into us from a very young age. I distinctly remember developing the habits of judging and complaining in my early teens at the influence of a former boyfriend. These habits of complaining and judging were then perpetuated through continuous conditioning within my community and social groups, through peers, elders in my life and the media.

Just watch the news; really pay attention to the content with fresh eyes and you will see exactly what I mean. The news stories that are negative could be delivered without the added hype. Often, news stories are inaccurately skewed in favour of drama and negativity. It is also rare to encounter news stories that are alerting people to the joyous occurrences in the world. I was of the belief that the saying 'no news is good news' meant that positive news stories do not exist on the television (and who can blame me?). I have only recently discovered that the saying actually means, 'if you don't receive any news, it means that all is well.'

You are exposed to a culture in which a major way of communicating and connecting with others is through complaining. Complaining is the opposite of appreciating and it is nothing more than a habit. You already intrinsically know what you like and don't like. You don't need to highlight, focus upon and obsess over the things that you dislike.

Acknowledging that which is not working is an important step in making positive life changes, however, this differs from complaining in that it is not enshrouded in negative energy. Instead, it is a sober recognition that it is time to create something different with an emphasis on what is preferred. Once you have recognised that you don't like something, resolve to change it, let it go (emotionally) and shift your focus towards your desire.

Solutions rarely come when you're in the midst of emotional turmoil. There is a tendency for your thoughts to become unsettled, erratic and irrational if your emotions have become out of balance. Winning solutions do not come through a troubled mind. If you are attempting to find a solution whilst in the grips of negativity, do your best to calm yourself down first. Diverting your attention to something uncomplicated and in the present moment, such as awareness of your body and breathing, can help you reconnect with that calm space within. It is from this quiet and calm space that your answers will suddenly happen upon you.

This is where learning to appreciate is of tremendous value. When you catch yourself feeling tense, notice your thoughts. It is likely that you will find some form of complaint, inner resistance or denial of a circumstance that you find displeasing. If there is nothing that you can do to change the circumstance, then this is a perfect time to practice diverting your attention.

Take some time right now to list some things that make you feel instantly calm and happy when you think of them. You can use these things later if you need help to change your mood. Better still, set yourself up for the day ahead by taking five minutes before you arise, to think of things you appreciate. It could be your garden, your friend's baby, a niece or nephew, your child, a pet, a peaceful spot in nature, a holiday you once had, a funny moment in time, a loved one or a charming building. It could be absolutely anything. Every day, take some time,

Practice Appreciation

even if it's just five minutes, to write about, state aloud or think about things that you appreciate. Maybe you love how good you feel in your body, the sunshine, your freedom. Maybe you enjoy your home or the city you live in. Perhaps you have lots of friends you love. Maybe you like that you can purchase something luxurious. Or perhaps you enjoy sitting and appreciating the sensation of your breathing and your heartbeat, the warmth in your body and the feeling of the connection with that quiet and peaceful place within.

If you take time each day setting yourself up and reconnecting with a feeling of magic and wonder, then you will find that magical things begin to happen. But if they don't happen, it doesn't really matter because it *feels* like magical things are happening anyway!

If you notice your mood dipping during the day, then take it upon yourself to think of things that make you happy or do something you enjoy for five minutes. Breathe consciously, journal, go for a walk, have a coffee, stretch, listen to some music, give yourself a quick massage. Just take five minutes to clear your head and reset into a good-feeling and appreciative place. Think of it this way: if you were to get a flat tyre, you wouldn't then continue to drive. Ideally, you would stop and change the tyre. If you were to keep driving with a flat tyre, eventually you will end up driving on a metal rim, sparks will fly up everywhere and the journey will be anything but relaxing.

If you practice appreciation and magnetising your emotions to a positive and expansive place, you will begin to notice things that feel good more often. Wonderful feeling ideas will occur to you more and more. Your timing will be exceptional and you will just know the places to go to and the people to meet. You will find yourself moving from one fun and satisfying experience to the next fun and satisfying experience and life can be like this even within the most ordinary of circumstances.

You may find yourself appreciating things that were previously unappealing and you will begin extracting the best from those circumstances. People will respond differently to you and they will be playful and fun to be around. Even people that you haven't traditionally had fun with will respond more favourably to you, simply because you are looking for things to appreciate within them.

Learn to appreciate life and watch your world transform. From within that space, you will be the most magnetic and glorious person. Your ideal lover will see you and adore you and won't be able to resist you. And when they do come into your world, you will love them all the more because you have learned how to appreciate. You will treat them with the love they deserve because you will cherish them and all that they have to offer you.

Chapter 12

Affirmations

Affirmations, if used correctly, can be a powerful tool for bringing anything wanted into your life. There is a common misunderstanding with affirmations that you are to rattle off statements that aren't necessarily true, in order to try and make it so.

While this can work when you are in a state of deep relaxation, such as during hypnosis or meditation, it may just be really frustrating to try and conjure positive statements if you're not feeling so positive to begin with.

Affirmations are best used when you are already feeling amazing or if you find limiting beliefs that you do not consider to be true and gradually reframe them in a way that is more suited to your desires. This is a skill that takes practice but once you get the hang of it, it's going to go a long way towards creating the life of your dreams, as well as attracting a partner into your life.

For example, let's say that you don't believe you deserve to be with the partner of your dreams because you don't feel good enough. Saying, 'I am good enough for my ideal partner' or 'I am worthy of the lover of my dreams' may be helpful at some point, when you are already in a good-feeling place but let's see if we can start where you are now and make the journey from there.

I will now demonstrate a self-coaching process that you can use to incrementally move into a better feeling place using true statements. You could say;

'I may not feel good enough at this point in time but I know consciously that this is just a bogus belief I have picked up along the way. This is understandable given the life that I have led. I'm working on feeling differently and I'm making steady progress. It's only a matter of time before this belief begins to shift for me. I know of some people whose worth isn't apparent to me and yet they have found lifelong partnerships, so there is some evidence to suggest that you don't have to be flawless in order to be worthy. In fact, the ideal partner in my life will believe that I am worthy, even if I do not believe it. I don't have to justify my existence or the things that I desire. I am invaluable to the person of my dreams who adores me unconditionally. I am worthy. I am good enough. I know this and I will come to know it more and more, as I take the time each day to shift my thoughts and coach myself towards that which feels the most harmonious.'

In this example, you are gradually moving to a good-feeling place where you are now in a position to deliver your positive affirmations. This exercise is about acknowledging exactly where you are (briefly) and moving to a new place using beliefs that are also true.

When you are feeling negative, there is always a part of you that doesn't buy into the reality of the emotion. You can call upon this wise part of yourself to assist in this process and to help show you what is true.

A belief only becomes a reality for you when you have practiced it enough to see evidence of it in your life. If you believe that people 'always' reject you, then you will be attracted to people who are going to reject you (or only focus on behaviours that indicate rejection, rather than noticing where you are being accepted) and so you will affirm this belief even more.

Becoming aware of your beliefs can be particularly useful in hastening your spiritual evolution. Observing the world around you and noticing how you interrelate with it can help you to hone your understanding of your innermost beliefs. This is the true meaning behind the concept that 'the world is your mirror.' What you notice and give your attention to in the world and what you are drawn to will be highly influenced by your inner state and your subconscious beliefs.

If you notice any limiting beliefs appearing in your world, you can use this self-coaching exercise to gradually soften these beliefs and then, ultimately, you can shift them.

Once you are in a good-feeling place, you can use your affirmations, that is, short, positive statements that are framed in the present moment, to help amplify your new beliefs. If you notice a limiting belief, write it down as 'What I currently believe is true.' Then write 'What I would like to believe is true.' And write down what you would like to believe instead. Then write your belief down again and ask yourself, 'How can I view this differently?' How can you view it in a way that brings you some reprieve from the negative weight that it has previously carried? Little by little, you can write a statement that feels slightly better each time and before you know it, you will be on a role towards writing the exact statement that reflects the belief you wish to hold.

Another time to use affirmations is when you're already feeling amazing. In fact, this is the most effective time to use them. In this case, a positive statement is made (quietly or aloud, depending on your preference; a written statement is also potent) that is framed in the present moment. For example, 'I feel so lucky right now' or 'I am the luckiest person alive.'

If you would like to continue on a positive affirmation tirade because it feels so good, you could say;

'I keep noticing the most beautiful things happening all around me at the moment. My timing is absolutely perfect. I keep showing up at just the right time for the most fun and exciting moments. I keep catching my friends and colleagues at the best of times and in the best mood and I am just so impressed by how fabulous my life is becoming. I am beginning to feel so joyful most of the time and things are always working so smoothly for me. Everything is becoming so easy and so fun and everything is working out so perfectly. I am really enjoying watching my life moving in this way. I am loving the blissful moments that are showing up and the exciting and delightful things that are surprising me in the most unexpected ways. I really like knowing that as I shift my beliefs and as I focus on feeling good, there are so many wonderful things coming into my life. I am beginning to feel so much peace and so much love and appreciation for life. I am feeling so complete. I am beginning to fall in love with life and my heart is glowing with appreciation. I am feeling so complete now; it is as if I don't even need a lover to come into my life. There is so much love in my life already and I love that people are drawn to me. Exceptional people, happy and joyful people have been drawn to me and I just love the fun that we have and the sharing and joy and laughter that occurs. It is just so good to feel good. I feel as though I have everything I could ever possibly wish for, just because I am feeling so happy, so fulfilled and so complete. This is incredible, that all I have needed, all this time, was simply a shift in my perspective and I have so many marvellous tools available to me to help me enjoy this process. I love my life so much. I love the simple joy available to me. I love how in love I am feeling. I just know that the person of my dreams is here within my heart, connecting to my heart and I feel as if they are already here with me. In fact, I know they will find me at just the right time and for now I am so in love and when they find me, oh wow! It is going to be so amazing! It will be so joyous and I am so excited for when that time comes. And for the time being, I am going to make the most of this time of self-exploration and spiritual growth and expansion because I am enjoying it so much. I am enjoying my life so much and I am so excited for what is to come.'

So, there you have it; an example of affirmations to use when you are feeling great and when things are going well for you. That is the perfect time to go on a rant about all of the pleasing things in your life. Affirm what is good and make the most of it. And if you're not feeling so great, you can use the self-coaching process to gently shift your beliefs into ones that feel a little better and a little better, until you're where you want to be.

Another thing I should mention here, is that it is okay if you're not feeling at your best every minute of every day. Don't worry too much if you find yourself falling into a funk once in a while. It won't ruin your chances of manifesting your dreams. You have plenty of chances with this and there isn't really a way to get it wrong.

How you feel is just a reflection of where you are in relation to where you want to be. Your feelings are simply showing you if you are on the right path with your thinking or if you're taking the scenic route to your desires. Either way, you don't ever really lose ground and you are never lost. You are always making progress towards your dreams because you are learning what it is that you want with every life experience. And one thing is for sure; you can't live life without having experiences!

Use your affirmations when you are feeling good and coach yourself when you're feeling not-so-good. Take the time to get into a good-feeling place as often as you can. Meditation is a highly effective way to shift your mood and an ideal time to use positive affirmations. Now, let's talk about meditation.

Chapter 13

Meditation

Where would I be without meditation? I shudder at the thought. I really do believe that in many ways, meditation has saved my life. When I was twenty years old, I had been experiencing recurring illness and a lot of pain in my body. I visited numerous doctors and not one of them could find anything wrong with me.

The final doctor I bothered to visit said to me, 'There is nothing wrong with you; you are perfectly healthy.' I was dismayed at this statement, as I had been feeling terrible for months on end. Several months later, a blood test revealed antibodies for glandular fever, which explained all of my symptoms but at the time, I was unaware of this.

I left the doctor's office and thought, 'If I am perfectly healthy, then my symptoms must be psychosomatic.' Feeling somewhat deflated and desperate for answers, I decided to see a psychic who was working out of my local

'Hippy Shop' but the lady at the shop advised me that the psychic was fully booked.

Seeing my frustration, she enquired further. After telling her of my 'psychosomatic' health issues, she suggested I could go to her sister's meditation class that was held weekly in a space above the shop. I knew immediately that this was exactly what I needed and so I went to that class. I went to that meditation class every week for five years and it completely changed my life!

I remember the first session I had. The meditation instructor guided us in a group setting through some lovely visualisations but I knew I was trying too hard to 'see' things in my mind's eye and I wasn't particularly relaxed. So, I resolved to let go completely and just relax in my next class, without trying too hard to make anything happen.

During the visualisation of my second meditation class, the instructor guided us to a water feature in a picturesque garden. I 'knelt' at the edge of the stone pond and 'gazed' at my reflection. The instructor then said, 'But you're not alone.' Immediately, the reflections of two figures appeared beside my own reflection.

One of the figures was feminine, completely luminescent and white. She was glowing and had large points of white light, like four points of a star, radiating from her torso. The points of light could easily be mistaken for the wings of a butterfly or an angel! Yes! An angel! This is what people see when they see angels; radiant beings of light!

There was also a masculine figure to my left. He had straight brown hair cut in a 'bowl cut' around his forehead. They 'told' me their names. I heard the name 'Michael' clearly, as if spoken inside my mind. The feminine figure was something beginning with 'H' that I had never heard before, which I translated to mean 'Harmony.' I later learned that her name was Haniel.

Before I knew it, Michael had faded into the background and my head was in the lap of Haniel, who was comforting me, transmitting the purest energy I had ever known. Here was this, literally awesome, being of light, holding me in the most positive regard and the highest esteem. For the first time in my adult life, I was feeling absolute and unconditional love. For the first time ever, I was finally able to just let it all go. I cried and cried. I had never felt such love, such adoration, such reverence.

After the meditation was over and when I had been brought 'back up,' I moved for the first time since the beginning of the meditation and every joint in my body cracked! I even felt the tiny joints in my hands and feet crack! And finally, I was free of pain and tension for the first time in months! It was rather extraordinary.

During the customary group debrief, the meditation guide asked me to recount my experience. I told her of Michael and of Haniel. She asked me about Haniel, 'What did she want you to know?' I thought about it for a moment. 'What did she want me to know?' and as soon as I became aware of the message Haniel had intended for me, I began to cry again. I replied through sobs of tears, 'She wants me to know that I am loved!' This was a simple, yet powerful message that many people today don't have the opportunity to experience fully.

Suffice it to say, I was hooked on meditation from that moment forward. And so it was that my meditation journey began. For a while, I was always hoping to recreate that incredible experience and it was only once I released my attachment to recreating that feeling, once I was able to stop craving that feeling, that I was finally able to progress with meditation.

Once I could settle into my moments, let go of expectations and 'go with the flow' a bit more, my meditations brought all kinds of insights and healing. I attended not only this class, where visualisations were offered but also present moment awareness meditations of the yoga tradition and Vipassana meditation courses.

Why would a person seek so many meditation experiences? Meditation will help you to learn who you are. It will help you to relax. Through meditation, you will heal physically and emotionally. As you practice, you will become more sensitive to your inner knowing and your preternatural discernment. Meditation reinforces your ability to recognise the messages of your inner guidance and make decisions in accordance with this guidance. Meditation helps you to grow and evolve as a human being. It helps you to become 'enlightened,' that is, lighter and happier. Meditation can help you to be successful. It can help you *fall in love* with yourself and fall in love with life. It can help you to feel love and to know what love feels like. Through meditation, you can influence your subconscious mind, creating habits and beliefs that serve you in order to manifest your desires.

My healing journey has been a long and arduous one but yours doesn't have to be this way. You can be happy, you can travel light (without baggage) and you can be drawn to other people and situations that mirror this. Meditation can be an invaluable tool in this process.

We have all been conditioned (at least to some degree) by Western society to think and believe certain things. We don't even question many of these beliefs because they are so 'normal' but that does not mean that a belief, however normal, is correct for you or is serving your highest possible good.

Meditation can help you to become aware of and gain access to beliefs that are ingrained in you but do not serve you. There is a common belief in Australia that is significant in holding people back in relationships, that is barely even questioned. This belief has its roots in the strict work ethic that is expected of people functioning within Western society and this is the belief that you 'must work hard to earn your keep.'

Animals are born free. They belong to the land and are literally made of the land. They are abundantly provided for. They have food, they have shelter and they have water. They are always connected to their creative source. They are present and they are loved.

Human beings are always loved. We belong to the land and are literally made of the land. We are abundantly provided for and we are born with everything that we need for a magical existence. But some of us are then told that we do not have the right to inhabit the land we walk upon, we are told that we must be educated in specific ways, we must pay money for water, we must pay money for food, we must pay money in perpetuity to have the right to a piece of land to belong to.

To achieve these monetary payments, we must get a job and be busy working most of our lives. Some people find work they would happily do forever and so if you are joyous in your work, then this will really suit you. If you are one of the people who does not love your work, then this will pose a significant challenge. Nevertheless, it is expected that we must *earn* our existence.

Working hard is highly regarded, while 'slacking off' or being an 'aimless drifter' is synonymous with having failed. Our society as a whole rarely questions these cultural norms. These conventions are the result of inherently flawed conditioning and are out of alignment with the Universal laws of creation through joy and inspiration. Subsequently, we learn that we not only have to earn our existence materially, through the monetary system but we must also work hard to earn other non-material acquisitions, such as love and affection. But love is not to be earned. Love is at the core of all life and it is what remains when the false layers are stripped away.

Now, here is another belief that is hardly questioned, that incidentally benefits a consumerist society. In the past (and I hope that these sales techniques will change, moving into the future) your purchasing choices have been manipulated by many means, one of which, is to make you feel that you are not enough, unless you purchase a specific product. As in, your identity will suffer in some way if you do not make a particular purchase to enhance your self-image, for example.

This is where the beliefs 'I am not enough,' 'I am not worthy' and 'I must work hard, struggle, strive and earn in order to have anything worthwhile' come from.

With these beliefs deeply embedded in the hearts and minds of many, it is only natural to feel that you should be, have or do something extraordinary in order to be worthy of the love of somebody extraordinary.

This is a very normal side-effect of the way Western society has evolved. These are very *normal* beliefs to hold but they are incorrect. You were born *worthy*. You are already extraordinary because you are a miracle. Your existence is a miracle. You are unique.

There will never be another human being like you on this planet and even if you have a twin or a sibling who is similar or identical to you, you are still your own person.

You are a unique perspective. You are a manifestation of the Divine.

You are extraordinary and there is somebody on this planet who will see you one day and think, 'Yes, this is the person I have hoped for. This person is the one who gets me. This person is the one who has all of the intricate quirks I have dreamt of. This person is the one I connect with and have fun with in a way that has never happened before. I am so thankful that they exist and I am so happy that I have met them.'

Yes, you! You are the one for someone. You are perfect. You were born perfect. You were born deserving of all that is good. Don't let an unconscious society tell you otherwise. You are worthy of all that is good. And this is a new belief that you can embrace fully, if you so choose and meditation can help you create this new belief.

I highly recommend seeking a meditation class or accessing the many online resources available. But if you would like a simple meditation to begin with, it can be a good practice to set aside some time each day and set a timer for ten to fifteen minutes to meditate.

When you do so, choose a comfortable position and make sure you will be warm enough, as the body tends to cool during meditation. As you sit or lie down to meditate, close your eyes and turn your attention inward. Bring your awareness to your breathing, without trying to change it in any way. The aim is to observe without drawing conclusions and without the commentary of the inner mental dialogue. Your mind may try to comment or may try to draw your attention to its thoughts and this is perfectly normal. If you notice that your mind has wandered, simply bring your attention back to the awareness of your breath.

Notice the movement of the rib cage as the chest and abdomen expand and contract with each breath. Notice the subtle movement of the collarbones with each breath. Notice the warm air on the upper lip as you breathe out and the cool air on the upper lip as you breathe in. Simply watch and notice your breathing. And keep bringing your mind back, gently, to the awareness of the normal, natural breath.

You may notice feelings arising during this time and if you do, again, simply acknowledge these feelings, allowing them to be there, without judgement and bring your awareness back to the breath. Keep your awareness relaxed and easy, as you gently return your focus to the breath each time.

When you are feeling relaxed and peaceful, it is an ideal time to say a positive affirmation silently to yourself. Make sure that it is true and make sure that it is a short, positive statement that is framed in the present (refer to the previous chapter).

If you are attempting to meditate and you find that the mind is very noisy, that's okay. The mind will eventually become quieter and meditation will become easier with practice, so it is good to have a go for a short while each day. Alternatively, you could try meditating at a different time of the day or perhaps after vigorous exercise, as this can sometimes help to quiet the mind.

This breath awareness meditation can be a good starting point but I recommend trying different styles of meditations, such as guided visualisations, as you may find them more suitable. The breath awareness meditation that I have suggested, with practice, will improve your present moment awareness and has enormous transformative potential. By simply observing the breath and the body without judgement, most often, old negative emotions that have been lodged in the body will come to the surface. These past grievances will be transformed when you can observe them without offering any resistance. This is a powerful way to release any negative emotions and beliefs that may be impacting upon your life experience.

When you meditate, however, be sure to allow your experience to unfold as it will, without expectation. I have never had the same experience of meditation twice. Every meditation is different and some will be more powerful than others.

Practiced over the long-term, meditation in general will help you gain mastery over your mind, learn who you are at a deeper level, understand your emotions and learn the difference between the emotions that you feel in your body and the deep inner knowing that comes from your intuition that is guiding you.

Chapter 14

Take Care of Yourself and Your Appearance

Sure, this may seem a little superficial but there are actually powerful reasons for taking care of your appearance and health. Why? Because it helps you to feel more confident and attractive to your ideal partner. If you like how you look and if you believe that you are magnetic, you will project this out into the world. You will have the appearance of being attractive to those who genuinely 'see' you.

In the long run, looks will fade and it would be wise not to base your relationship on looks alone. But appearance can change as you get to know a person. Have you ever met identical twins and you couldn't tell them apart at first? And in time, as their personalities and lifestyle preferences have emerged, they have become so obviously different that you can't understand how you ever got them mixed up in the first place?

Likewise, I have met plenty of men who appeared very attractive at first glance but as I have learned more about them, their physical appearance has actually seemed to morph and they have appeared much less attractive to me. The opposite has also occurred.

You will ultimately perceive who a person is on multiple levels as you get to know them, which will influence how they appear to you. Therefore, physical characteristics alone won't necessarily weigh heavily in selecting a mate. Nevertheless, your physical appearance will still form a part of what your other half will be drawn to.

One thing I like to keep in mind and experiment with, is the idea that 'beauty is in the eye of the beholder.' In Quantum Physics, the widely debated Observer Effect, suggests that an observer can affect the outcome of an experiment based on the act of observation. There are many theories that attempt to explain this phenomenon. However, based on the outcomes of numerous experiments, it would seem that reality is subject to the influence of the observer. Even if any mystical assertions are debunked in relation to the Observer Effect, this still has significance in terms of the *perspective* of the observer and the influence of their understanding of the Universe.

The field of neuroscience has proved the subjective nature of human perception on a number of occasions. But it is the functioning of human eyes and the mechanisms through which an image is formed that I find most compelling in terms of evidence for the subjective nature of our visual reality.

Much of what we 'see' is actually visual construct that occurs in an area of the brain, known as the visual cortex. This area of the brain forms an image that is based on a collective history of our life's experience and our interactions with the physical world. The actual real-time data that is received by the human eye is limited. This is why optical illusions are so effective, as they exploit this conditioning of the human mind based on its interactions with the physical world.[1]

I have kept this in mind with my own physical appearance. I thought, 'what if my appearance is just an illusion and what if I can project something much more youthful and beautiful to the world based on my belief? And if the world is a mirror, then what if I look for the beauty in all others? Will all others then see me as beautiful?'

I have been told on many occasions that I look much more pleasing in real life than what a camera can capture, so I think the projection of this illusion actually works! Just don't believe what the camera tells you! I mention this here to open your mind about what it means to be beautiful or beauty-full.

If you see your world as beautiful; if you have presence, love and peace in your heart, then you will be one of the most magnetic and enticing people in the world and your physical looks will not even compare to the magnetic radiance that you truly are. But your appearance can and will shift to mirror this inner magnificence. There will be those people who will 'see' you and recognise your worth.

But back to your health and physical looks. You must revere and take care of yourself as though you are worthy of the greatest love and care available in this Universe. You can't just think, 'what's the point? There's nobody to love and appreciate me; nobody's going to see my nether regions, so why bother taking care of them?' Well, you can think that. You can think whatever you want. But such an attitude is in opposition to the manifestation that you would like to create. It does not value yourself, your magnificence and your true beauty. It effectively hammers in the message to your subconscious mind that you are stuck in singledom.

How do you take care of yourself? Get the right amount of sleep for you. Find ways to relax. Make time for doing the things you love. Be active with things that excite you. Make sure you lead a productive life but make sure you also have time for leisure. Eat foods that are in harmony with your body. Engage in physical movement that enlivens and enriches you. Find clothes that represent your personality and that you feel comfortable and happy in. Groom yourself and tend to your personal hygiene. Use products that are in the best interest of your health. Do what is right for you.

I strongly recommend making sure that *you* feel good about how you look. Nobody else matters. It is important that you appear the way you wish to appear and that you

Take Care of Yourself and Your Appearance

are attractive in your own distinct way. Your perfect partner will be able to recognise you more easily this way.

Before I had the premonition about meeting my soul mate, I was never particularly concerned about what eye colour, hair colour, height or build a man was. If I found him appealing, I found him appealing. Once I had the premonition, however, physical characteristics did become significant to me. In my dream, he had olive skin, blonde hair and blue eyes. While I still dated men who didn't fit this description, in my heart, I knew that the man I was going to be with did.

So, I prepared myself for his arrival. I worked towards improving my physique by getting active and eating well. I selected a style that pleased me. I continued to be self-reflective and to grow. I became the person I wanted to be; a person who I felt was worthy of this perfect man of mine. It has helped a lot. It helped me with my confidence and self-esteem and it helped me to feel like a good match for the man of my dreams.

Since we finally met and started dating, it has even helped with my confidence within the relationship, even though, (and he will vouch for this) he actually doesn't care in the slightest how I look! He somehow sees the real me and thinks that I am beautiful, regardless of what state I'm in. I like to joke that it can be really annoying when I want some constructive feedback on how I look before we go out somewhere. The answer is always; 'You look beautiful' but I think it's best not to complain about these things.

So, you're not really making any changes for anyone other than yourself. And if you're pleased with how you look, then own it! Allow yourself to be confident. I've had somebody tell me they take great pleasure in dressing themselves in clothes that they feel represent them. This person was literally glowing and looked absolutely gorgeous. It was very apparent that they took great joy in the ritual of tending to their appearance. When telling me of this, they suddenly recoiled and became self-conscious, in case I thought they were conceited.

There's a significant difference between being confident or conceited. In Australia in particular, I'm afraid we don't allow people, especially women, to be confident enough. So many people dim their light and act meek because they want to be liked and they don't want to make anyone jealous. Please shine your light brightly! We need more people to shine! When you shine your light brightly, you will inspire others to be their very best as well. The jealous people will just need to learn to deal with it and discover their own worth.

If you find yourself falling victim to jealousy, it is a sign that you want what somebody else has and that you're comparing yourself to them. Do your best to bring your attention away from the comparison if you can. It also helps to imagine yourself there, purely as a witnessing presence. Become present (anchored in your body) and from that space, celebrate the person in front of you. See their beauty, their energy and their radiance and keep your thoughts on what it is that you love about *them*.

Take Care of Yourself and Your Appearance

Resist the temptation in your mind to compare. If you do this successfully, those very people will be enthralled with *your* attractiveness, as you will be projecting your adoration of them.

Withdraw your attention from those who do not support you in your thriving. Allow yourself to shine and be beautiful, that is, filled with beauty. And men, I am talking about you as well. Yes, you too, can be beautiful and it is preferable to aim for this (inner radiance and magnetic charm) over trying to look a certain way through extreme behaviours and a sense of inadequacy.

Take care of yourself and take care of your appearance as though you are deserving of the most wonderful blessings this world has to offer. As you focus on your inner light and radiance, as you allow this to emanate from within you, you will attract the right friends and the right people, who are happy for you and support you, as you grow into the person you have always wished to be. And you will attract a partner who adores you, exactly as you are.

---

1. David Eagleman, *The Brain: The story of You* (Pantheon, 1st Edition, 2015)

Chapter 15

Live Your Life as You Imagine it to be with Your Ideal Partner

For a long time, I was pining for my one and only, my other half, the one who would complete me. And during this time, I forgot how to enjoy life. Luckily, at some point, I finally decided to just live my life and embrace all the 'good' that was already available to me.

But before I made this decision, I had to discover what it was that really made life worthwhile. I knew I wanted a man who was passionate about nature and the outdoors, who was healthy, adventurous and active. I had an inkling that my ideal man was an ocean lover, since that is where we met in my dream.

I was in love with the ocean and often fantasised about surfing, although, having grown up inland, I didn't really see this as a reality; just a fantasy. But then, my circumstances changed and I experienced an unexpected and massive upheaval. It was only then that I decided to make a change. It was only when something horrible had happened and I had left my old life behind that I finally decided to make my fantasy life a reality. I was being presented with an opportunity. Why not move to my favourite holiday town on the coast? Why not live in the place where I spent all of my childhood holidays? Why not become a coastal dweller?

I had a feeling that when I moved to the coast, I would meet the love of my life. And I had a feeling that my ideal partner was a surfer. I met him in my dream by the coast and he had blonde hair and tanned skin. He just had to be a surfer!

In my mind, if a person lived at the beach, they had to surf. Why wouldn't you? Well, that was just my opinion at the time. And so, when I moved to the coast, learning to surf became one of my priorities. I was terrified of waves but after my first session alone (on the best beginner waves I've experienced to this day) I was hooked! That magical day, the best day of my life until that point, was enough to carry me through the fear and challenges that surfing presented for years to come.

Surfing became my passion. I fell so in love with it that I would often find myself sitting on my surfboard in the ocean thinking, 'I am so in love, I do not even care about having a boyfriend right now.' I dated people after I started surfing and all of the people I met were surfers, except one.

Dating that one non-surfer made me realise I could only ever be with a surfer because only a surfer understood the passion, the love, the joy, the intrinsic need for and calling to the waves. I very much enjoyed going on dates that involved surfing and coffee. I imagined this would be a favourite thing to do with my ideal partner, so I embraced these as my favourite activities to do alone and with friends.

During this time, I discovered what was important to me and what values I wanted to share with my ideal partner. I would envision my life with him and I would carry out my days as though I was already with him. I became concerned at one stage because my life was so perfect that I didn't want anything to change! I made a rule that I wouldn't commit to a man unless he allowed me to feel as happy and in love as I already felt.

By living your dream life, the way that you want it to be when you have your ideal partner, you are telling the Universe that you believe. You are matching the energy frequency of that which you wish to attract into your life. You will feel a sense of completeness, so much so, that you won't desperately need that person to come into your life. When you don't *need* your lover to come this very moment, then you won't desperately cling to and effectively repel any would-be suitors.

You will be living your dream life and if that person comes, it won't matter. And if they don't come, it won't matter! It won't matter because you are happy already! This will place you in a much stronger position than waiting for your partner before you start truly living because you won't settle and you won't compromise.

When you are happy already, you won't settle for somebody who doesn't mirror your happiness. You won't settle for somebody who doesn't share your passion for life. You won't settle for somebody who doesn't admire and celebrate you. You will wait for the perfect person because anything less simply won't do, as you already have everything and are living the life of your dreams!

So, imagine what your life will look like when you have your perfect partner. Does it involve romantic dinners? If it does, then have a romantic dinner at home alone. Set the mood with some soft lighting, some candles and inspired music on a quality speaker. Cook a sumptuous dinner for two, if you like (you can eat the leftovers tomorrow). Dress nicely, as though your lover were there with you. Revel in the blessedness of the moment. Be present. Accept the moment as perfect. Feel the love, life and joy in your body. Taste and relish the deliciousness of your meal.

Imagine your life as though your lover were there with you and accept your moments as being worthy of your happiness. This will expedite the arrival of your lover but also, it will help you embrace your moments fully. After all, life is but a series of moments, is it not?

There was one vital mistake I made early in my quest for great love; I made my happiness depend on it. I allowed my emotions to fluctuate and my self-worth to be built around whether a man was attracted to me. For many years, I did this unaware.

If only I had known that I could feel complete without him for all those years, I wouldn't have habitually denied my moments. Don't let your moments go to waste because you have deemed them 'unworthy' of your happiness. Each moment is sacred, perfect and precious. When you find this sacredness, you have found all that you need. Your partner will come at the right time. Just be sure to treat your time in between with great reverence.

Chapter 16

Falling in Love is Just Chemicals in Your Bloodstream

When I was a teenager, my dad had often said, 'Falling in love is just chemicals in your bloodstream.' My first impression was that my dad was just cynical. Since I was raised in an era (a very long era, that is) of Disney princesses and rom-coms, I was inclined to be a little more romantic than my very pragmatic father.

Since I didn't really have enough information on the subject, I kept an open mind. It wasn't that I was inexperienced romantically at that stage, I just didn't have any way to prove or disprove what my father had suggested.

In my late teens, I discovered a passion for soccer and played a season for a high-ranking team in my local area. However, my soccer career was short-lived. My aspirations were shattered when a knee injury took me out of the competition just before the finals. A surgeon recommended that I should have an arthroscopy to tidy up the injury and fully assess the damage. This was back in the days of pre-meds. I believe the purpose of a pre-med was to ease the patient into the surgery prior to the anaesthetic by relaxing them but I actually think that my anaesthetist may have got a kick out of playing with people! My pre-med was a real eye-opener!

The anaesthetist put something into my cannula and whatever he gave me made me extremely anxious. I was instantly in a state of sheer panic! But because I had felt the injection go into my hand and travel up my arm (until the solution became warm) I knew that the emotion wasn't real. I spoke rapidly through shallow breaths, 'Whatever you just gave me made me really anxious! Could you please fix it?' and then he immediately reached for another syringe and injected it into my cannula. I was calm at once. It was like I had been at a day spa every day for the past week and I didn't have a care in the world.

This peculiar event intrigued me but my curiosity would have to wait. I was just happy to bathe in the blissful feelings I was experiencing. The anaesthetist then gave me something else (the general anaesthetic) and I vaguely remember him asking me a bizarre question, at which point I contorted my face in confusion and that was all I remember. I imagine the effect was rather comical to the medical staff present in the operating theatre. I'm sure they all would have had a good laugh about it.

This may have been slightly unethical but I didn't mind at all. The experience was quite fascinating to me and showed me something significant. It showed me that my feelings (not to be confused with intuition) are not always that reliable. And yes, it meant that my father was right!

Sometimes, what you feel is just the result of chemicals in your bloodstream. If you've ever been hangry (the result of being angry due to hunger) you will know exactly what I mean. It can be somewhat perplexing to note that as soon as you eat something, there is no problem at all. When just moments earlier, you thought the world was about to end because of some (minor) disaster.

This doesn't mean that what you feel is meaningless. It is good to be aware of what you feel. It is good to acknowledge your feelings. However, it is best to refrain from immediately buying into the reality of your emotions, without further exploration or more information. Acknowledge what you feel but do so with presence, without judgement and without drawing any conclusions, if you can.

In the context of a romantic relationship, chemistry with another human being is certainly important to a degree. But it is good to keep in mind that it isn't the *only* critical factor in selecting a mate and that what you feel may purely be a chemical reaction in your body.

When I first thought I had fallen in love, it felt so amazing and I was completely smitten by my boyfriend. I was fourteen years old at the time, so quite naturally, I thought my life was over when he ended the relationship. I thought he was the only boy who would ever make me feel that way and I was doomed to be alone forever or settle for somebody I didn't love. It felt like the biggest disaster and like my heart had been ripped out.

I was so very wrong to think that he had been the only one for me. And as I look back now, I know that he was not even close to being the right person for me. We had the most exhilarating chemistry and it was that chemistry alone that led me to believe I had found something special. But he was just a teenage boy wanting to be with a teenage girl in the way that many teenage boys do.

While chemistry is a substantial factor in choosing a mate, it isn't the only thing that matters. There are many compatibilities to consider. If you have chemistry with a person you're interested in but they also come with a myriad of deal-breakers, then it would be good to hold off on making any commitments to that person.

When the chemistry subsides to a nice and steady pace as the relationship matures, it is advantageous to have things in common with your partner and to have something much deeper to sustain the relationship.

If you can connect with the deep, peaceful aspect of your inner self, then you will be in a much better position to recognise when you have found a person with whom you have a deeper connection. This space within is also the place from which your wise inner guidance arises. It is from this place that you can connect with the truth of your being; a truth that is beyond the turmoil of any emotions.

How do you recognise when you are listening to your inner truth? Learn to sharpen your awareness and be present. How do you learn to sharpen your awareness and be present? Read my chapter on meditation. It will help.

Chapter 17

Take Up a Hobby that You Love

If you tend to be a clingy type of person, then it could be beneficial to take up a hobby that you love. This is because the more a person 'clings' to another, the more the other is repulsed.

What exactly is being clingy? Being clingy is when you are holding on tightly to another person because of fear of losing them. And why does this happen? If we were to look at the much broader perspective of this tendency, you are most likely going to cling to a person when you subconsciously sense that they aren't really that into you. Feeling insecure and grasping at them will only affirm this and push them away.

You won't be consciously pushing the other person away but they will sense that your happiness and self-esteem depend on whether they like you and this is naturally repulsive.

I've seen lots of people trying to 'play it cool' and seem aloof in order to do all of the right things but this doesn't work because somebody either likes you, or they don't. If they don't want to be with you, it doesn't necessarily mean that there is something wrong with you. It simply means that perhaps one of you is being more honest than the other. It means that the other person recognises something is amiss between you and they aren't prepared to compromise. Don't be offended. Be happy that you have ruled out that person as an option. Each one who isn't 'the one,' brings you closer to 'the one.'

Wouldn't you rather sense that somebody isn't into you, be realistic about it, be self-assured, secure, balanced, independent and enjoy your time together? Is it really the end of the world if they aren't that into you? And if you don't trust yourself not to cling to somebody, (and by this I am referring to the unhealthy *energy* of negative and insecure attachment to another) wouldn't it be beneficial to have something in your life that completes you and makes you feel whole?

Wouldn't it be great to have a distraction that makes you feel good? So instead of sitting by your phone waiting for that next text message from your latest love interest, you're out having the time of your life and your happiness no longer depends on whether or not they want you.

Now, we could become really advanced here and stipulate that your happiness need not depend on anything outside of yourself at all. Through your meditation practice, you could find lasting peace and happiness. This need not take a long time. You can find this peace and happiness right now. But if you consider that you are still in the process of becoming enlightened, then why not be proactive in finding a sense of completeness by utilising the extraordinary things around you that life has to offer?

Look for things to feel good about in life. Keep an open mind and try new things. You may find something that you absolutely love and that makes you feel a sense of completeness and a knowing that 'yes, I am exactly where I need to be right now. I am the luckiest person alive and I would not change a thing.' When you arrive at this feeling and when you are there often, you will be in the ideal state for meeting a deeply satisfying partner.

When you are in this state, you will feel so complete, you will know that you do not need another person to be happy. You are happy and complete already. Oh and there could be a really lovely side-effect of finding a hobby that you love. Getting out there and engaging in a new activity or hobby can be an excellent way to meet like-minded people. And while it is possible that this could be an avenue for meeting your ideal partner, I don't advise engaging in a hobby purely for this reason. This is something that you must do only for yourself and then if you do meet someone, consider it a bonus.

For me, the activity that brings a feeling of serenity, completeness and connection is (you guessed it) surfing. Surfing and my love of the ocean complete my heart and soul more than any other human could. It is for this reason that I knew I preferred a partner who is a surfer. I wanted to be with somebody who would understand the magnetic pull to the ocean and would prioritise this activity, just as I do.

But you may find your mojo elsewhere. I encourage you to go out and explore your world. I encourage you to consider the things that you have always wished you could do. Use your imagination to consider engaging in those activities. Do some research about your interests and find something that excites you.

I am not suggesting that taking up a hobby is a compulsory step in finding the love of your life. But if you are open to the possibility, it could be a good avenue for you to create something in your life that you are passionate about and that gives you a sense of completeness. That way, if you end up dating somebody who isn't that into you, you can just front up to the relationship, be candid and enjoy at least making a new friend. When you decide to part ways, that person will have a positive memory of you; an independent, passionate and interesting person.

And wouldn't you rather allow people the freedom to choose? Wouldn't you rather be genuinely secure and awesome, so that you are magnetising people to you and you are the one who is being selective?

A new hobby that you love could give you the confidence that you need. A new hobby could show you new skills and strengths that you didn't know you had. A new hobby could help you make new friends who will show you just how amazing you are. A new hobby could give you a sense of joy, love and a zest for life that you didn't believe was possible. A new hobby could make you revel in your life experience and feel a greater sense of appreciation. A new hobby could make you irresistible and draw the most extraordinary person into your life. I think a new hobby could be worth considering, don't you agree?

Chapter 18

Don't be Afraid to Say a Quality 'No'

Are you the kind of person who is very concerned with the feelings of others and not comfortable with being responsible for hurting other people? And if you really don't want to attend a social occasion, even though it means a lot to somebody else, what are you inclined to do? Do you just go along with it anyway, politely agreeing, despite not wishing to partake?

I have ignored my gut instinct on several occasions just because I was taught to be polite. I have gone out on dates when I didn't want to and I have spent time doing things I knew I didn't want to do.

Now, it is possible that you can make the most of a 'bad' situation and agree to have a good time regardless of the circumstances. But sometimes, a person might ask you out and you just know that you're not interested in dating them. Do you go along with it anyway because you don't want to hurt their feelings?

If you don't see a future with a person, the fact is that your time with them has an expiry date and there will come a time when you will have to say 'no'. The question is; how long are you going to wait before you tell them you're not interested? How many dates will you go on before you let them know they are not the one for you?

Learning to say 'no' clearly and without reservation may seem harsh but you may also be sparing a person some long-term embarrassment and you're not wasting your time or theirs. You're actually doing both of you a favour, even if they cannot see it at the time.

And yes, there are some people who will try to make you feel bad for declining their advances. There are some people who will act angry and hurt in an attempt to manipulate your feelings. This only confirms that they are not the kind of person you wish to spend time with.

You want to be with somebody who is secure enough to allow you to exercise your free will and your own decision-making, don't you? If a person feels the need to manipulate your feelings and play on your good will, then they are demonstrating their insecurity, dishonouring you and not respecting your boundaries.

It is vital for you to learn to say 'no,' especially if you do not wish to be alone with a person. You are not obliged to put yourself in a situation that you are not comfortable with because a person is not mature enough to handle rejection. There are billions of people on this planet and an adult who is on the dating scene will have to face rejection at some point. Don't be afraid to say 'no' to the ones you do not wish to date.

When I was in my late teens, I had a close friend who would go out to nightclubs with me on the weekends. She was very kind and polite and didn't like saying 'no' to me. There was one time, when she made up an excuse, that was obviously a lie for why she wasn't able to go out with me.

I called her out on the lie and told her, 'It's okay if you don't feel like you want to go out. I understand and I know that you still love me. But in the future, I would prefer if you're honest and just tell me you're not in the mood to go out. I don't expect you to always say 'yes,' you know?' And so that is precisely what happened. The next time I phoned her, she said, 'I don't really feel like it.' It was confronting for me at first but I valued her honesty and we opened the doorway for an open and authentic friendship that has lasted many years. Even to this day, while we are worlds apart and living our own separate and busy lives, we are still good friends.

It is good to have people in your life who appreciate your situation, consider your needs and demonstrate genuine empathy. If you are always feeling as though you have to tread on eggshells around a person, your relationship with them will lack authenticity and you will not be able to be yourself around them.

There will be times when you will want to do things for friends because you know it will make them happy. This is the most benevolent expression of love and generosity of spirit. But in these instances, you will do something because you care about the person and how they feel, not because you feel manipulated.

In circumstances of dating that involve your safety, you must learn to say a quality 'no' if you are not feeling safe. Don't just go along with it and put yourself in a situation with a person you don't know very well, if you don't feel safe.

I once had a much older man chat to me in a busy beach car park and I was polite and friendly towards him. There were other acquaintances around at the time and it was all very jovial. After a few laughs, the conversation ended and I proceeded to change into my swimmers. I bundled up my towel and headed to a secluded section of beach that I was planning on swimming and sunbathing at.

That was when I noticed that the man had followed me. He then tried to engage me further. I was polite but I made it clear that I was no longer interested in talking with anybody, saying that I wanted some 'time to myself.' He became furious and started yelling at me and telling me I was 'rude,' which was a very unhealthy overreaction; an overreaction that suggested I was right in feeling uncomfortable.

Sensing that I was in danger, I immediately walked back to the busy area of the beach. This man was trying to manipulate me into feeling guilty in order to satisfy his agenda. I refused to believe that I was rude and I refused to be concerned that I had upset him. My reason for being there was to relax and enjoy some time alone. I am not obliged to be there to entertain a stranger who followed me to a secluded area without an invitation.

Even to this day, I am not remotely concerned that this man was angry. He can call me 'rude' and call me as many names as he likes and nevertheless, I am not concerned. Did I make him angry? Or was he making the choice to become angry because he didn't get what he wanted from me and because he believes that throwing a tantrum is the way to get what he wants? Unlike that man's parents, I don't reward tantrums and bad behaviour.

It is nice to extend generosity and kindness towards others. But some behaviour is not appropriate, such as, following a young woman to a secluded section of beach and yelling at her when she is not obliging.

Be polite and kind to people in public areas, where you are safe, if you wish. But remember that you are not responsible for the feelings of others when they are behaving improperly towards you.

You can be an uplifter and help others to feel good when it is right to do so. But if a person is pursuing your affections and you're not comfortable with it, you absolutely have the right to say 'no'. You can say it in a way that is polite, of course.

You can say something clear and polite such as, 'I don't wish to go out with you but thank you for asking.'

Remember that you do not need to justify your quality 'no' or provide an explanation. You know in your heart if spending time with a person (romantically or platonically) is right for you and you don't have to justify it.

Don't be afraid to back yourself and your decisions fully. It is impolite for another person to disrespect your wishes, so don't let anyone manipulate you into feeling bad for honouring your truth. If you need to learn to say 'no,' then it may help to practice with family or with a close friend who you know will still love you, no matter what.

As you refuse to be involved with the ones who are not right for you, you keep yourself available for the ones who may be right for you. You listen to your heart, respect your own wishes and empower yourself. You give yourself the best opportunity to find people who also respect and empower you.

You deserve the very best and you do not need to settle for less than you deserve. Say 'no' to the ones who are not right for you and only say 'yes' when you know that you'd like to spend time getting to know somebody.

Chapter 19

Forget About Meeting Your Soul Mate!

Yeah, so, you know that book you've just read? You can go ahead and forget about all of that now. Just kidding! I hope you consider the content you've just read to be an invaluable contribution towards your quest for love. But really, once you are wholeheartedly enjoying your life experience, you will still be incomplete in the sense that, for some individuals, there remains a powerful drive to connect with another human being on a physical level. It is perfectly natural for the opposite energy polarities to feel drawn to one another. This is the nature of spiritual and sexual energy and the energy of creation.

You've probably heard the saying that 'Life is what happens when you are busy making plans.' It is a reminder that if you focus too intently on what you wish to achieve, your determination for your future goals can overshadow your moments. The most fundamental thing in life, however, is to inhabit your moments.

In the personal development industry, goal setting is a big deal because how terrible a fate it would be if you were to be an 'aimless drifter!' I'm being facetious, of course. I don't agree with this. While I do understand the value of setting goals, I am also acutely aware that life can sometimes take unexpected twists and turns and so, it is vitally important to keep the majority of your attention in the here and now.

Life isn't happening yesterday and life isn't happening tomorrow, it is happening now. The quality of your moments now determines the quality of your future moments. This isn't referring to your life situation, however. Your life situation can always improve, no matter how bad (or good) things may seem. What this statement is actually referring to is your ability to be present and appreciate your moments. As long as you are seeking fulfilment in your future moments, you will continue to seek fulfilment in your future moments. That is because the future cannot come. When the future arrives, it will do so as a now moment.

If you are habitually denying your now moments because the future is looming, you are effectively squandering your moments of life that are being offered here and now. So, learning to embrace your now and allowing your now to be a high-quality moment, will be a significant investment in your ability to enjoy your future moments as they arrive, here and now.

Being in the now doesn't mean you suddenly have your memory wiped and you're incapable of planning ahead and foreseeing likely outcomes. You can still reminisce and learn from past experiences and you can still make plans. But when you do so, it will be advantageous to maintain at least some of your awareness in your physical apparatus, that is, your body.

Why? Wouldn't it be a terrible shame if you were so driven to achieve a goal, that you didn't enjoy the process and didn't inhabit your moments, allowing your life to pass you by? And usually, a person who is so driven will achieve their goal but because they haven't learned to inhabit their moments, the happiness that arises is fleeting. Before they know it, they're onto the next goal and the next, without ever stopping to savour their experience or celebrate the attainment of their goals... and then they die.

But I deliberately said 'they' because I am not referring to you. This is not your fate. You will be aware of your desire and your goal to be in a deeply satisfying romantic relationship, while at the same time making the most of your life, exactly as it is right now.

You will let go of your attachment to the outcome because you know that your beloved is on the way to you; you have absolute faith that the future is assured and you can just relax and enjoy what life has to offer.

In making the suggestion to 'forget about meeting your soul mate,' I am recommending that you let go of the driven obsession that can sometimes occur when pursuing a desire. This is the habit of thinking that tells you 'I am too busy to have fun right now. I will be happy and have fun when I am done working towards this substantial goal that I have.'

There are those who say, 'It will happen when you least expect it.' This is because some people will hold fast to their goals with an unhealthy intensity and attachment to the outcome. When such people let go of their attachment to the outcome (when they relinquish expectations) that is precisely when their manifestation occurs.

I liken this to a phenomenon that occurs at the bow of a boat. When the boat is moving forward with intensity, any flotsam at the bow is pushed away by the wake of the boat. But when the boat eases off the throttle and drifts forward slowly, the flotsam will be drawn to the boat and will make contact with the bow. Likewise, when you ease off on the intensity of your desire, rather than pushing it away, it will be drawn to you.

When the intensity of a desire is amplified to the extent that your wanting becomes a brutal reminder that you have not yet achieved your goal, you are effectively pushing your goal away. If thinking of your soul mate reminds you that you have not yet found them, then it is best to keep your thoughts away from the subject for a while. Come back to the topic only if it amplifies your positive feelings of being in love.

The key to manifesting your soul mate relationship lies in amplifying your positive feelings. These positive emotions do not have to be in relation to the topic that you wish to manifest. If you can tap into the *essence* of what you wish to feel as a result of your manifestation, then this alone is enough for things to begin to shift for you. Forget about meeting your soul mate and amplify your feelings of being in love, enraptured and joyous!

Remember, when you have met the love of your life, you will most likely be together for the rest of your lives. That is (hopefully) a really long time. Don't be in such a hurry to escape your current situation. There is significant value in appreciating your life as it is right now. Enjoy being single and enjoy this precious time of getting to know yourself and how glorious you are! When you recognise how superb you are, when you fall in love with your life, exactly as it is, it may not be long before you are united with your other half.

Chapter 20

Foster Positive Friendships

Spending time in the company of those who love you unconditionally will go a long way towards remembering how loveable you are. If you are experiencing loneliness and you do not know many like-minded people, then you must find strength and peace within your current situation. I will address how to do this shortly.

Wanting to find a romantic partner out of loneliness can cause you to compromise on the type of partner that you allow into your life. Have you ever had a significant other in your life who was less than you wanted? Was the relationship abusive, manipulative or volatile in any way? What was your reason for deciding to enter into or remain in that relationship? Have you ever ended up in a relationship that has been less than you deserved because you felt lonely?

Being in the grips of loneliness can make you vulnerable to the wrong types of romantic partners and friendships.

When you learn to soothe these feelings of loneliness, you harness a certain strength that puts you in a position of exercising your freedom to choose.

Being alone does not necessarily mean that you will experience loneliness. There is great strength in being solitary and some people will actually prefer it. When you are by yourself, you do not have to confer with anyone in order to make decisions. You can have everything just as you want it to be. You can allow your mind to become still and you do not need to engage in conversation. Being alone will offer you a tremendous opportunity to experience peace and quiet. Do your best to look for things that you enjoy about being single but if all else fails, there is another way to enjoy your solitude.

If you do find that loneliness is visiting with you, it will be helpful to bring your attention deeply into the present moment. See if you can bring your awareness into your body and focus on your breathing for a short while. This need take no longer than five minutes, so commit yourself to this exercise now. Just close your eyes and take three deep, conscious breaths and allow your mind and attention to remain on the breath. As you allow your awareness to rest on your breath, see if you can notice the inner body, that is, the essence or the energy that animates your form. See if you can notice the arising of presence.

As you practice presence, the mind will become still and there will be an arising of peace. As this peace begins to arise, a sense of deep content can also emanate from within. As you connect with this spaciousness within you, a sense of completeness will become apparent. You will begin to know your connectedness with all other beings. When you know your connectedness and your oneness with all of life, loneliness cannot possibly visit with you. Practicing presence and practicing meditation can alleviate any sense of loneliness.

Have you chosen to be alone because you have refused to compromise by spending time with people who do not suit you? Then you are sending a signal to the Universe that you are not willing to settle for less than you wish for. This is an affirmation of your strength and tenacity towards the life of your dreams. When you feel complete and secure and when you know your worth, you will attract new and remarkable people into your life. Find ways to enjoy being alone and make time for activities that you love. You will eventually find those who reflect the marvellous person you are becoming.

If you are a social person and you have friends that are all disappearing because they are meeting their soul mates and dissolving into their little love bubbles, then listen up. You need to be very careful with your energy right now. If you are feeling annoyed or angry that your friends are prioritising their romantic partners, remember that you are also going to meet your soul mate.

Do you want your friends to be annoyed at you when you are disappearing into your love bubble? Do you want to enjoy your time with your friends as a couple once you have re-emerged into the world and are ready to socialise again?

Before I met the love of my life, many of my friends and acquaintances started meeting their life partners. They suddenly disappeared and I found myself doing a lot of things alone. I thought to myself, 'Okay, I am doing things alone right now and that's fine. One day, I will meet my guy and I hope my friends forgive me for wanting to spend time with him.'

I refused to be negative towards my friends for suddenly disappearing and spending most of their free time with their new lovers. I was celebrating their newfound happiness and I was really excited because I knew it would be my turn one day soon (it took about another twelve months thereafter).

So, if your friends are disappearing because they are meeting their twin flames, don't be mad at them and don't worry. They will re-emerge and will be excited to spend time with you. Also, it is a sign that your turn is coming!

The best friends are those who support you as your life takes twists and turns for the better, so it is good to offer them the same courtesy. Don't burn your bridges. Just meet new friends or enjoy spending time alone until your friends are ready to hit the social scene again.

If your friends are all still single, then enjoy the bonds and the friendships that you form. Enjoy the activities that you love doing together. Speak of your dreams and remain positive. Support one another as you make desired life changes. Spend time predominantly with those people who accept you exactly as you are and are happy for you as you become who you wish to be.

I personally like to have friends who challenge me and differ from me in many ways. I do this because it helps me to grow and because I genuinely see value in these people. But if you are feeling tentative in your ability to manifest the life of your dreams, you may like to focus mostly on the friendships that are harmonious and uplifting for a while.

When you are enjoying the company of like-minded individuals who uplift and support you, you will remember how loveable you are. You will relax and have fun, enjoying leisure and laughter. You will feel satisfied and joyous in the knowing that there are others out there who reflect back to you the joy that is in your heart.

You will learn what you love about yourself, what you love about your interactions with others and your individual talents and skills that others appreciate. You will learn of your value and what you have to offer as a friend. You will discover what ignites your passions and gets you fired up. You will hone your social skills and build confidence in your ability to connect with others in meaningful ways. Oh and you just may, through a friend of a friend, meet somebody very special.

Your relationships with your friends will be valuable, not only during your single life but also as you spend time with your beloved. Your friends will offer variety and perspective. Your friends will bring a certain fun and playfulness that you will enjoy during and beyond your relationship with your romantic partner. Your friends offer a certain connectedness and appreciation that can last a lifetime.

They will add to your growing family of adults as you all meet your partners and connect with one another at various times. Enjoy the support and companionship of your most uplifting friends and appreciate their existence in your life. They will walk beside you as your life evolves through its various stages and can add meaning to your experience of this marvellous dance of life.

Chapter 21

Coping with Rejection

Anybody who has ever existed on this planet has probably experienced some form of rejection. Being afraid of rejection is a perfectly natural response if you have been rejected in the past and found it to be a painful experience. I'd like to remind you here that rejection comes not only in the form of romance. People can experience rejection within multiple contexts. Fear of rejection can inhibit your ability to manifest love if it prevents you from going out on a limb to find something that is desired. If a past rejection has caused you pain and is preventing you from moving forward in your love life, you may like to read on.

If you have experienced romantic rejection and you are now suffering from it, then it means you are personalising the rejection, that is, you are making the rejection into a personal problem.

Being rejected does not mean that you are a failure, nor does it mean that you are not good enough. It simply means that the person who has done the rejecting does not consider you to be a suitable match for them. That is all. If you go on to make a story out of the rejection thereafter and give it more meaning than it deserves, you will hold yourself back from finding a partner who is perfect for you.

You won't always know the reason for being 'let go'. In fact, oftentimes, you won't be given a reason that is plausible. Sometimes, the best explanation is that you just weren't compatible with one another. Even if a person does give you a reason for not wanting to pursue a romantic relationship with you, it may not be the absolute truth. And it doesn't really matter.

If a person does not want to be with you, they don't owe you an explanation. They have the free will to decide the future of their romantic life, do they not? You wouldn't want a romantic partner to manipulate or coerce you into being with them, would you? Nor would you want a person to be with you against their will.

Remember not to make it personal. Remember that there is at least one person out there who adores you, just as you are. If you like yourself as you are but a prospective romantic partner doesn't like you, then why should this person's opinion dictate how you feel about yourself? If a person you like does not feel the same way about you, then it is best to let them go. Even if they have all of the qualities that you wish for in your ideal partner, there is still one quality missing that is glaringly obvious and it is a big deal-breaker. They don't feel the same way about you. They cannot possibly be perfect for you in this one respect. If you cling to this person, even after they have told you they do not see a future with you, then you are affirming a scarcity belief that something better cannot come along. Do your best not to get hung up on a past rejection.

If a person has refused to give you an explanation and you have been obsessing over various scenarios, potential reasons for the rejection or things that you may have done wrong, then you will need to do your best to apply discipline to your thoughts. Without further information, you cannot possibly know what that person thinks of you. Even if a person tells you what they think, it isn't always accurate.

Sometimes it is possible to perceive explanations differently to what they were intended, especially during emotionally difficult circumstances. It is best not to jump to conclusions about how you are perceived by others. If another person doesn't want to be with you, it doesn't have to be seen as a rejection, nor does it have to be taken personally.

If a person doesn't like something about you that is fundamentally who you are, then being hurt or attempting to change that particular trait will only hide you from the person of your dreams. Trying to change for those who do not love you will make you unrecognisable to the ones who do love you.

On the other hand, if you receive constructive feedback on something you would like to change about yourself, then it might be worth considering. Let's say an ex-lover tells you they didn't like how you 'always had to be right and win arguments.' If you decide, upon reflection, that this is something you would like to change, there is no harm in taking this feedback into consideration. But what if somebody were to say that you talk too much and upon reflection, you realise that talking is how you express yourself when you're happy? If it's something that you do like, that is quintessentially who you are in this lifetime, then don't change it. You will find a partner who appreciates that you talk a lot when you're happy.

Make sure that you measure any perceived rejection against your truth and your own preferences. Don't put yourself down because one person doesn't want to be with you. Don't even put yourself down if many people don't want to be with you. The good news is that you've had the opportunity to get to know many people in the first place. At the very least, you've had a number of people who were interested in exploring if you were potentially the one for them. This is a sign that you are alluring to begin with.

And if there is only one person out there for you, then knowing who is *not* for you is ruling out the non-viable options. If you can simply say, 'I guess they just knew before I did, that we were not right for one another' rather than taking it to affirm a negative belief you may hold about yourself, then you can be much more efficient in the dating process.

If you find that you are getting hung up on past rejections and making them into a narrative about your life or who you believe you are, it can highlight negative beliefs you may have. Any self-discovery in life is priceless and can help you to evolve as a human being. Here are some common negative beliefs to look out for;

- It's only a matter of time before they leave me
- I am too old
- I am not loveable
- Nobody would want to date a single parent
- I am unattractive
- I can't see how I could possibly meet somebody in this town
- I can't find a person who is willing to commit
- They only want one thing
- Real love is hard to find
- All the good ones are taken
- I don't deserve love/I'm not good enough
- All of the single people in this area are rude
- I have nothing to offer
- I will end up alone
- I'm always second best
- If they find out who I really am, they won't like me

Please note that this is not an exhaustive list and you may find something entirely different from what is mentioned above.

The essence of all negative beliefs is the same. They involve you making sweeping generalised statements, as if they are fact. They stem from turning your thoughts to a dark place that does not feel good, in response to an unwanted event, in this case, a break-up or rejection.

If viewed from a positive perspective, you will discover that your negative beliefs have been formed to serve a positive purpose in your life, such as, to protect you from harm. You can always look at a negative belief or behaviour in terms of what it is attempting to achieve *for* you. When you understand the positive purpose of the belief, you can reconcile those parts that you may have previously denied. There is enormous power contained within any fragmented subconscious aspects of yourself. As you shine the light of your awareness upon them, they join forces with your intent and form a part of your powerful manifestation arsenal.

It is good to be aware of and consolidate any false ideas that you hold about yourself and your dating life. You can change any negative beliefs in time and it may be helpful to see my chapter called 'Rectify Negative Self-Talk'. If a rejection helps you to identify a negative belief, then it has served an important purpose. It has helped you to find something that you would like to heal as you move forward on your journey towards meeting your soul mate.

Bless all of your experiences that you are having right now because each moment and each event is drawing you nearer to your manifestation. The longer you remain hung up on a past rejection, the longer you keep yourself unavailable to the love of your life.

Don't let somebody from your past tell you that you're not good enough for true love, just because you aren't the one for them. Don't make it into a false belief about who you are. It can't work out with every person you meet. That would be completely impractical. If you have been rejected, then remember; you are now one person closer to finding your beloved and your beloved adores you, just as you are.

Chapter 22

Observe Other Couples and Relationships

After I'd had enough of dating as though I were a pinball in a pinball machine, aimlessly bouncing from one prospect to the next, I became more proactive in working out what I wanted in a relationship. But because I had limited examples of inspiring romantic relationships in my life and had no experience of a healthy relationship myself, I had to look for examples elsewhere.

As soon as I began looking for examples of what appeared to be harmonious soul mate relationships, I began seeing them everywhere! You can imagine my surprise then, at being confronted by my own negative emotions when I first started noticing these couples.

I would have thought that it would please me to see other couples but in fact, I was reluctant to accept the couples that were showing up in my life. They had what I wanted, so I was refusing to allow them. I was envious, as the couples were reminding me of what I wanted but didn't yet have.

A good way to navigate the feeling of envy is to briefly acknowledge the feeling and its message; that what you are observing is something you wish to have. If you feel envious of somebody for anything that they have, don't dwell on the negative emotion associated with it. Instead, use it to reaffirm your own desires.

Feeling envious can help you understand the *essence* of what you want. Once you have recognised this, or if it is not an issue for you, then you can begin to notice and observe the other romantic relationships that you see manifesting around you.

The possibilities of romantic partners and relationship dynamics are about as varied and endless as there are unique individuals on this planet. It is beneficial to observe other relationships and couples in your life to get an idea of what you want in your own relationship.

You may even find a couple that inspires you and provides an example of exactly what you wish for. In these instances, it can affirm for you that the relationship you dream of is a real possibility.

With this exercise of observation, you are essentially looking for evidence that your manifestation can be real and that truly happy and fulfilled couples do exist. You are also getting an idea of what it might look like, should your ideal person walk into your life.

Observe Other Couples and Relationships

Intend to see examples of couples that genuinely light one another up. Intend that you will notice examples of couples that bounce off one another and live together harmoniously. Intend to look for couples that are happy, healthy and living an expansive and satisfying life.

When you do see these couples appearing in your life experience, notice how it makes you feel. You will know you are ready to meet 'the one' when you can see these great love relationships and they excite and inspire you. When you notice examples showing up in your experience, thank the Universe for these signs and signals and know that what you wish for is on its way to you.

Observe other couples in your life. Learn what your preferences are. Use these examples as evidence that your great love relationship is on its way. You will know that it is on its way to you because when you see examples, you will feel blessed and in love. You will be genuinely happy for the couples you observe. You will feel excited and inspired. You will feel a sense of peace, joy and completeness. You will feel as though what they have is already yours in essence and you will just know that your very own perfect version is already on its way to you.

Chapter 23

Rectify Negative Self-Talk

Rectifying negative self-talk is an essential component of creating lasting positive change in your life. This is something that requires you to be aware of your feelings, as your feelings will alert you to any automatic negative thoughts or beliefs that you may hold about yourself and about your life situation.

It will require you to be alert to your thoughts but this can sometimes be an exhausting task, especially if you have a lot of negative self-talk that you wish to be aware of. A good way to approach this, is to be aware of how you are feeling and if you repeatedly notice a particular negative emotion, ask yourself 'is there anything that I am thinking right now that is contributing to this feeling?' or 'how might my thoughts be contributing to this negative emotion?'

It is imperative that you are not too hard on yourself as you go about the process of rectifying any negative self-talk because, well, being hard on yourself is more of the same. More often than not, simply noticing the thought with awareness and not taking it too seriously will be enough for it to begin to resolve, as you are not adding more energy to it or giving it any reality.

I cannot possibly know what your inner thoughts are but I can provide an example of a common belief that hinders people in finding happiness and accepting the extraordinary circumstances they deserve. A common example is the belief that 'I am not good enough.' If you hold this belief, then it may very well be that you notice the person of your dreams, only to quash your desire immediately with a thought such as, 'Oh but they are way out of my league. They would never be interested in me.'

When you meet your ideal person, you will most likely think that they are the most incredible person on the planet, really. And you are good enough for them. In fact, you are absolutely everything that they have ever hoped for. You must not discount yourself or your self-worth. So, if you see a person who you think is amazing and you desire to date them, simply notice your thoughts and feelings about the subject.

When you are ready to date the person of your dreams, you will feel secure, confident, joyful, playful and easy about the whole process. If you are feeling anxious or nervous about approaching a person, either you intuitively sense that something is amiss, or you're not yet ready to believe that you deserve the absolute best. Don't

Rectify Negative Self-Talk

worry, you won't miss out. Take some time to be ready. Keep noticing your thoughts and feelings on the subject.

Meditation will help you notice your actual feelings and affirmations can assist you in creating new, positive beliefs. To briefly reiterate; affirmations are short, positive statements framed in the present such as, 'I am worthy of love.' Affirmations are best stated when you are feeling good, so simply notice your negative self-talk. Don't try to change any negative self-talk right away. One of the most potent times to state your affirmations of what you *do* want is during or after meditation.

Notice your negative self-talk or beliefs with a sense of curiosity and without judgement, if you can. You do not have to get to the bottom of these thoughts and beliefs or understand their aetiology. There is no need to analyse them. If you can notice with curiosity and simply be aware, you can gain greater insights into the thoughts and beliefs that have been shaping your life experience thus far. It will give you a keen awareness and a new understanding of how to proceed as you move towards shaping the life of your dreams.

A good way to move out of negative self-talk is to treat yourself as a beloved friend would. This involves some self-coaching, especially if you are feeling particularly negative or anxious. If you can speak kindly to yourself, just as a friend would, you can begin to soften and change the negative self-talk and you can gradually feel better about all that you are and all that you have created.

You can either do this in your mind, out loud (preferably in private, since society doesn't look kindly upon those talking to themselves!) or by writing a letter to yourself. Writing to yourself from your source of higher wisdom, or a wiser part of yourself, is an effective way to gain insights and to soften any harsh thoughts or beliefs that you may have.

Make sure that the new thoughts you are creating are not outright lies but instead, stem from thoughts that you can accept as the truth. For example, you may not believe that you are nice-looking and this may be a 'truth,' based on the subjective nature of what our society considers to be nice-looking. A positive version of this belief that represents the truth, is that you are most certainly *attractive* to the right person. If, however, you cannot possibly accept this (or other negative beliefs) as a truth, then it may be best to avoid the subject. If you notice a negative emotion relating to this belief arising, then think about something that you love. Think about a pet that you love, children you adore, the ocean or your favourite holiday. Daydream about the chemistry you will share with your ideal lover or anything else that helps you to feel good.

Another way to feel attractive is to take the focus off yourself. Instead, focus on the other person and their attractiveness, without making any comparison. In my early twenties, I was spending a lot of time with a good friend of mine who worked as a fashion model. Suffice it to say that she was absolutely stunning! She was acquainted with many of her equally exquisite-looking colleagues.

Rectify Negative Self-Talk

I felt inadequate and self-conscious whenever I would spend time with my friend and her fashion-savvy acquaintances. But at some stage in spending time with her, I noticed that my feelings of insecurity were inhibiting my ability to enjoy her company. I knew that I had to do something about my feelings, as I didn't want to waste my time spent with her on negative energy.

I came up with the idea of simply focusing on how gorgeous my friend and her acquaintances were. I decided to completely remove the focus from myself and only focus on the beauty that I was seeing. It took practice and each time my mind was tempted to compare my appearance to theirs; I had to shift my attention to focus solely on the elegance before me. This practice was highly effective. I began to feel the most intense joy and appreciation at the beauty I was witnessing.

If you decide to try this out, you will view other people from the perspective of an observer and you will be there purely as a witnessing entity, perceiving others whilst revelling in their glory.

This is a really gratifying practice and once you take comparison and self-criticism out of the picture and delight in the appeal of others, you will be surprised at how often people will find *you* attractive. It is your energy, joy and the light that is in your heart that people find alluring after all and so there is no need to concern yourself with whether your nose is crooked or your eyes are too close together (in your opinion).

If you are unable to believe that you are attractive, then simply notice the thought and change the subject. Keep doing this as a practice and soon enough you will stay only with thoughts that feel good to you. There will come a time when suffering will no longer be acceptable to you and so you will quickly move your thoughts and your attention to that which feels good.

Remember, you always have the option to exercise your present moment awareness. If you can connect with the energy of your inner body, your physical body or your breath, as you do in meditation, you will free yourself of any negative self-talk and you will find the spaciousness within that is always there for you, should you choose to connect with it.

The more you practice this state of being, in pure awareness of your inner essence, the more easily you will find your attention drifting to this state and the easier it will be to feel good, irrespective of your circumstances. In this state of feeling good and being present, you allow things in your life to shift in a much more positive direction. If only you can allow yourself a little relief from negative self-talk, you will give life the opportunity to deliver to you that which your heart desires.

Chapter 24

Set Them Free

You've heard the saying, 'if you love somebody, set them free.' It's hard to know exactly where this saying originated but it clearly stands to reason. In any situation where you desire a manifestation, you will know that something is decidedly yours when you feel secure enough to release your attachment to the outcome.

Please note that this doesn't necessarily mean having an external, nonchalant attitude. When you relinquish your attachment to the outcome, you will release any *inner* resistance that you may have. You will allow your manifestation to come to fruition or not. You will not demand that life bends to your sheer will. You will maintain inner balance while allowing life to shift and flux around you. You will be steadfast in your knowing that what you wish for will be delivered to you in a most pleasing form.

It is good to keep an open mind about how your desire may manifest. Your desires and dreams won't necessarily be given to you in a specific form or even one single form. Sometimes, you will see your desire manifested all around you in various forms. If you trust life enough to enjoy and acknowledge the forms that do manifest in your world and if you allow things to move in and out of your experience, you will allow more of what you want to come to you.

When you are ready to receive your manifestation, you will know because you will understand that it is yours, no matter what. You will know that you do not have to cling to it, possess it, manipulate it, strive or struggle for it. You will know that it is yours and you will be aware of a sense of deep peace at the very core of your being.

You will know and trust that you can let go and allow things to flow effortlessly and easily into your experience. Your manifestation is yours and so it is that you do not need to force the course of events in the direction of your desires. That which you love will be drawn to you.

I must highlight here that the word 'love' in the English language is extremely limiting and does not fully encapsulate what it means to love. When you genuinely love another person or thing, it is without expectation or fear. When you love another, you will want that person to be happy, regardless of what that means for you or your relationship. If you sincerely love a person, you will respect their freedom and you will want what they want, even if what they want is not you. When you love, there will be a strong sense of peace and something wise and powerful in you that will surface.

Are you attempting to cling to, possess or control somebody out of fear of losing them? Fear is not love. It is the opposite of love. If you are holding onto a person who is not obliging because it was wonderful once or because it has the potential to be wonderful again, then you are not doing yourself any favours. You are holding on to an illusion, a memory or a projected and imagined future.

This is not valuing your present moment reality, the space in which your life is unfolding and the only place that true love can exist. You cannot miss out on this person if they are the one for you. Even if you are not together, you will feel a sense of peace and knowing.

If you are on edge or afraid at all, then you are not being loving towards them, the situation or yourself. Even if they are the perceived one at fault, you are committing a disservice and holding yourself in bondage by refusing to let go of the negativity.

If you want your situation to resolve miraculously, then you must find a way to let go. The letting go that I am speaking of here mostly involves letting go energetically. In some instances, you may still be able to maintain a relationship with a person and at the same time, let go of having an attachment to any particular outcome. You will allow them the freedom to live life as they please.

There have been many instances where only one person in the relationship has known, with absolute certainty, that they have found the one for them. If you do decide to pursue another person who is not yet convinced that you are the one for them, you must be sure that you are kind, gentle and flexible in your *energy*. Ensure that you are not being manipulative or holding a person to expectations that they cannot fulfill.

You must find a way to love genuinely if you would like to be free of negativity and if you want things to move in the direction of your desires. Being fearful is like telling the Universe that you do not trust. Being fearful and anxious is resisting your situation and not allowing the things that you wish for into your life experience. When you let go of fear and allow love into your heart, you are allowing life to deliver that person or something even better to you.

I've always made it clear to my partner that even if we are married, I do not expect him to always be with me. I love him with all of my heart and want him to be happy, even if that were to mean going our separate ways. I know that I have found my other half and I am deeply satisfied. I feel completely trusting of him, of life and of the Universe.

I have dated other people and with some I have felt uneasy within the relationship. But with my soul mate, I have never felt insecure about our relationship. If things were to end between us, I would no longer feel the need to search for my other half. I am satisfied in the knowing that if our purpose together has been served, then so be it.

I am in love with life. As an individual, I feel complete and blissful. I do not need to cling to my partner, nor am I dependent on him for my happiness. He is free to be with me or not. Together, we are happy but I know that the source of my happiness comes from a much deeper place within and so it is that we are free to love and be happy.

Before I met my current lover, I dated a man who moved away for work. By refusing to let him go energetically, I did him a huge disservice. I didn't let him know what I was going through emotionally and 'played it cool.' But in my moments alone, I was anxious, angry and hurt.

To try and cope with my emotions, I wrote a letter to him that I didn't intend to send and it helped me tremendously. I could sense that he was being affected by my emotional state and I was putting enormous pressure on him, in that my happiness and self-esteem depended on whether he wanted to be with me. I know that this was repulsive to him on an energetic level.

In hindsight, I know that this man was not a good match for me and I knew it from the very beginning. But intimacy with this person had clouded my judgement and better knowing. I am actually very thankful that we parted ways when we did. I appreciate the suffering our separation caused me because it led me to seek refuge in meditation.

The meditation process that I did for the next two weeks brought immediate relief and helped me to feel so in love with life that I was able to release him absolutely. I let go of my anger towards him for leaving and I felt joy at the memories and experiences we had shared. I was able to be loving towards him, even though I no longer had anything to do with him. I was able to fully and completely let go of my obsessive need to control the outcome. I had completely set him free. If he was meant to be mine, he would have found me irresistible at this stage. But instead, I became irresistible to the most extraordinary men. Releasing my attachment to the outcome and finding a centre of love within is exactly the energy that brought the love of my life to me.

Always seek to return to the centre of love that exists within you, even once you have found your soul mate. There is nothing in life that you can successfully possess forever. Physical life is subject to change. Physical forms come and go. Relationships begin and end. You can remain caught up in the seeming reality of this dance of life, which can make you fearful. Or you can find the love and peace that remains, always, beyond all physical forms. And when you do, you will know deep peace and you will know that nothing real is ever lost. You will stand firm in your unwavering state of peace and joy. You will allow the love of your life to come to you of their own free will. And when they do, you will love more boldly than ever before because you know that your union is inevitable, it is ordained, you have completely let go and so it shall come to pass.

Chapter 25

Ask Yourself 'Why Do I want to Meet the One?'

There are some goals in life, such as finding a partner, that are so socially acceptable that few people stop to question the validity or relevance of such a goal. This book has been written based on the assumption that you would like to meet the love of your life and 'settle down' into a monogamous relationship.

I would like to acknowledge that this kind of relationship is not for every person and that there are pressures from society which may play a role in influencing this desire for some people. It is therefore a good idea to ask yourself truthfully, 'what are my reasons for wanting to be in a relationship?' The intention behind this question isn't to get you to doubt your resolve or to put you off your search for 'the one.'

One intention of this question is to assist you in knowing and being comfortable with your reasons, so that you fully understand why you want your desire and can back yourself completely, without reservation.

It is time for you to thoroughly examine your goal and to be sure that you are ready. In doing this, you can be certain that your goal is exactly what you want and that you want it for reasons that are wholesome and acceptable to you. Another reason for scrutinising your goal is to identify any areas that you may need to adjust or realign with your truth.

This means that you may find reasons for your desire that don't match the truth of your being. For example, if you think that you 'should' find that one special person, simply because you are getting older, you may like to reconsider this and find a perspective that is less in alignment with scarcity (the time scarcity of growing older) and more in alignment with joy and what you will gain. Another way you could view your situation is that you have led an enriching life, enjoying the freedom of being single and you feel it is time to have a romantic companion to share your fabulous life with.

Let's say that you would like a lover in your life in order to be happy. It is vital to note here that while a person can contribute to your happiness, it will be wise not to expect another to make you happy. Becoming dependent on another for your happiness will cause an unhealthy, emotionally dependent relationship that is destined to experience difficulty, if not end soon after it has begun. In fact, wanting a person to make you happy will eventually lead to unhappiness and not achieve your intended desire.

Recognising that you would like another person in your life in order to be happy will be a sound way to open an honest dialogue with yourself. If this is you, then you will have some work to do. If you want a healthy relationship that brings happiness into your life, then you are more likely to succeed when you can achieve happiness independently of another.

'But I'm lonely! How can I possibly be happy when I am lonely?' Does this thought visit you at times? Then here is some good news; it is possible to achieve happiness on your own. Spiritually speaking and in essence, you are never alone. You are one with all that is. This oneness can be felt and known when you quiet your mind and bring your energy, attention and awareness intensely into the present moment. In this moment, you will know peace. In this moment, you will know contentment. In this moment, you will know a sense of profound completeness that is beyond all life forms, all forms of impermanence and that which is subject to change.

Even when you do meet your other half, it will not be forever on the level of form. It can and will be forever in essence, as the love you share is beyond this world. But everything that exists in the physical world will cease to exist in its present form in time. So, you cannot rely on any form in your world to make you happy.

If you can be content and be at peace prior to any physical manifestation, you will relish everything that comes into your life experience because you know that nothing is forever and nothing real can ever be lost. All that you essentially are, the essence of love within you, the sense of presence and being-ness, remains unchanged, always.

When you connect with this space within, you will know your wellbeing and your worth. You will allow life to move around you and you will remain centred in a state of joy. You will be able to love deeply, for your love will come from a sense of completeness. You will have real empathy and understanding for all other beings and you will not seek to control or manipulate another, nor will you hold the expectation that it is the responsibility of another to make you happy.

It is beneficial to become familiar with the essence of what you seek, so that you can create this energy in your life prior to the arrival of your lover. Aligning yourself with the energy that you are hoping your new partner will bring into your experience will, incidentally, expedite their arrival.

When you become familiar with your reasons for wanting a partner in your life and when you examine the energy behind those reasons and realign them with your truth, you will place yourself in the position of attracting a relationship that serves you on multiple levels. In other words, you are more likely to attract the right person.

Ask Yourself 'Why Do I want to Meet the One?'

If you want it to happen sooner, then you will need to be completely objective and make sure your reasons are not coming from a sense of lack, incompleteness, loneliness, obligation, time-scarcity, fear or boredom but instead from a sense of inspiration.

When you are living a life of joy, a life that is happy, fulfilled, authentic, free and fun, you place yourself in a much better position to find 'the one.' When you are living a life that you enjoy so much that you don't need a person to come into your life, you are much more likely to find that person waltzing into your life. When you are feeling inspired and excited at the idea of knowing a person who is thrilled with all that you are and all that you are living, you will be open to those who adore you. When you hold steadily to what you know to be true in your heart and feel a sense of lightness, ease and joy in your approach to dating, then you will know that you are ready for something special to enter your life.

Be sure that your reasons are aligned with joy, not with fear or lack. Write down your reasons openly and then find a way to capture the feeling that you are hoping to achieve through finding your ideal lover.

Meditation and visualisation can help you find the essence of what you are hoping to create through finding a relationship. You can use meditation and visualisation to conjure a sense of joy in life and connect with your inner sense of completeness, irrespective of your external circumstances.

Finding The One

When you align with your reasons for wanting a great love relationship and create the essence of this, when you feel complete and fall in love with life, you will become irresistible to the love of your life.

Chapter 26

Enjoy Being Single

Once you have met your other half, that is it. Game over. You may never ever be single again. Well, this is one possibility and it is worth considering. That means that yes, there will be fresh adventures and new experiences to be had as you embark upon your relationship. But the single game could be gone forever (or until death do you part).

Being in a relationship is potentially a very enjoyable and fascinating process of growth, companionship, friendship, creation, dissolution of forms, renewal, support, love, romance and self-discovery. Meeting my soul mate has been one of the most natural and easy things that has ever happened and I cannot imagine life without my other half. But it did dawn on me in the beginning that I would never be single, ever again. I was so deeply satisfied with my life when I met my partner that I was happy either way; whether he had walked into my life, or whether I had remained single. That isn't a bad thing but in hindsight, my only wish is that I had embraced being single with more fervour and I hope I can offer this insight to you, so that you don't miss out on what might be a very fulfilling time of self-discovery.

The irony is that the sooner you enjoy being single, the sooner you will most likely end up being in a 'couple'. But if you don't meet your other half right away, you won't really mind because you're too busy enjoying life and feeling deeply satisfied. This isn't an attempt to turn you off being in a relationship but I am going to have a go at getting you to be happy exactly where you are, right here and right now. Why? Because when you are happy right here and right now, that is when magic happens and not only in your romantic life.

Let's look at the positives of being single. Right now, as a single person, you have a great deal of autonomy and freedom. You do not need to negotiate your choices with others all of the time (only sometimes) and for the most part, you can do as you please, without concern for how this may affect a significant other in your life. When you meet your other half, it will probably surprise you at how much you have in common and how little you have to compromise on your choices. But you will most likely still factor them heavily into your decision-making process. So, for now, you can enjoy having complete autonomy. You also have the opportunity to know yourself to the core and to spend time alone.

If you are planning on meeting somebody and you have yet to start a family, you may find that 'me' time becomes a rare commodity down the track. So now is your chance to dedicate time to you! Really! If you can, use this opportunity to spend time alone doing things you love. Give yourself the attention, the expansion, the joy and the love that you need. Set aside some time each week that is dedicated solely to you. Use that time to be whimsical if that suits you. Or just use that time to do the things you really love but may have been putting off because 'what's the point' if you're doing it alone?

When I started going to cafés on my own in the early 2000s, I remember feeling somewhat awkward at first. The wait staff were often confused. They would bring over two menus, two glasses and a bottle of water and then leave me for a long time because they were waiting for the other party to arrive. I had to try and catch their attention early and say, 'It's just me' so that they would wait on me.

Dining alone has become more acceptable in the current time and it is a great way to get out, 'people-watch' and connect with the 'outside' world. It's also a great way to make some new acquaintances.

You do not need to let being alone deter you from going out and doing the things that you enjoy. It may feel awkward at first but you will feel more comfortable with it in time. And honestly, there is no need to feel self-conscious. People are rarely watching you and critiquing.

In my observation, people are mostly focused purely on their own experiences and perceptions.

So, enjoy being single in the best way that you know how. Spend time alone in nature, if that is what you love to do. Go to cafés and treat yourself. Have a date at the movies. Learn a new skill. Take up a new hobby. Exercise. Enjoy your autonomy. Live a life that is so enjoyable and so productive that you don't need the love of your life to enter your experience and having them with you will just be a bonus.

When you are steady and secure in your place of being single, you will allow potential partners to come into your life experience without the expectation that they will complete you, without ignoring vital signs that they are not right for you and without compromising. You will simply enjoy and bless their company and the feelings of magnetism that exist between you.

You won't need to cling to any one person because you will know that something better will come along, even if a person you're dating is almost (but not quite) right for you. When you enjoy being single and spending time in your own company, you will want to meet a person whose company you enjoy as much as you love being alone.

And when you meet a person you enjoy spending time with as much as you love being alone, you will know you have found something exceptional that has the potential to last a lifetime. Enjoy being single now. Your lifetime romance awaits you. Now is your opportunity to enjoy being single.

Chapter 27

Life After Meeting 'the One'

You may now live happily ever after... or so it would seem, according to Hollywood movies. If you have finally met the love of your life, you don't suddenly stop being an individual and you don't stop evolving spiritually. Life will still present challenges. In fact, the relationship itself may provide a source of rapid spiritual growth.

When I met my partner, I hadn't been in a committed relationship for a long time. It surprised me to note that the very act of being with a person on a consistent basis challenged me enormously, as did being with a much younger person. This raised many of my own insecurities surrounding both independence and attractiveness.

Being in a relationship with a person can be a trigger for emotional baggage to surface, especially if your past has been challenging in relation to romance. My mother was emotionally dependent on men who were violent throughout the majority of my childhood. I therefore struggled with the reality of being in a relationship, notwithstanding that my romantic relationship was an interdependent and harmonious one.

This was an overreaction to past trauma. There is nothing wrong with being in an interdependent relationship, where both partners support one another. However, there existed within me a deep-seated irrational fear that manifested when I had finally found somebody I wanted to spend the rest of my life with.

I also had to address my insecurities that surfaced, as a result of being eleven years older than my partner. I found myself questioning whether I was attractive enough for him. I also questioned the practicalities of wanting children, in terms of having different biological time-frames. This is a topic that is certainly worth sober consideration. If your partner has a different time-frame to you, it may be the grounds for the relationship ending, so it is good to know where you both stand on the topic. Since I was much older than my partner, I raised this concern with him very early in the relationship.

It is crucial to understand that meeting 'the one' does not mean that your issues magically dissolve. I experienced rapid spiritual growth when I first met my partner and it was phenomenal. The relationship-specific challenges that manifested amazed me and who better to work through them with than the love of my life? And throughout it all, he loved me unconditionally. I could be me. It forced me to be accountable because I now had a reason to be my best.

You will continue to grow when you meet your other half and they will often know exactly how to help you through it all. And if they can't help you through something, you will draw upon your own inner resources to overcome any obstacle because now you have a reason (other than you) to be your very best.

Because the relationship can be so enjoyable, magical and satisfying, there can also be a tendency to make that person your source of happiness. You will notice if you have inadvertently made your lover the source of your happiness because you will feel disappointed in them if they do not behave in a certain way towards you or satisfy your expectations of them. (Please note that I am *not* talking about abusive behaviour. If your partner is abusive or disrespectful in any way, regardless of whether they are your soul mate, it would be wise to question if this is the person you wish to be with and to seek professional assistance).

If you find yourself getting frustrated or angry towards a partner for not meeting unreasonable conditions that you have set out for them, then you are not being loving and you are making the other person responsible for your happiness. When you love somebody, you will be self-reflective, you will be transparent and you will admit if you have behaved in a manner that is unfair.

If you note that you have made your lover the source of your happiness, bringing your energy and attention back into the body and into the present moment will help affirm your ability to be happy as an individual. As soon as you do this, you will experience a sense of relief; any tension will dissipate and you will open the doorway for a resolution.

Remember the strong centre of peace and presence that is within. When you bring your attention to this space within, when you meditate or do an activity that brings you relief, you remember that *you* are the source of your happiness, not your partner. Being in an uplifting relationship with your soul mate will require you to balance reliance on them and reliance on your inner being to be the source of your happiness.

It is okay for an external circumstance to make you happy. It is just good to remember that you can still be happy, regardless of how that circumstance fluctuates and shifts. And your relationship will fluctuate, shift, grow and change. As human beings, you are dynamic and you are in a continuous state of becoming. Ideally, your partner will grow with you and you will support one another as you make your shifts, changes and new decisions.

But ultimately, your relationship with another will only be as good as your relationship with yourself. If you notice a shift in the dynamic of your relationship with your partner that is not desired, then take the focus off them and find a way to release the negativity from within you, before you address it with them verbally. You may find that it is no longer a problem for you or that it miraculously resolves, simply because you have let go of the negative energy or resistance to the situation. If the problem persists, however, then you will be in a peaceful state when you address it with your partner and you can have a constructive conversation.

Throughout reading this book, you have learned what it means to be happy on your own and to fall in love with life. This is the very energy that has drawn your other half to you. If you find that you are wavering at all within your relationship, then remember this energy of being in love. Remember your state of happiness and bliss that preceded your manifestation, that is, the meeting of your other half. This is the very energy that will sustain you, not only throughout life in general but also within your romantic relationship.

Remember always that you are two separate individuals that complement one another perfectly. Return to that centre of love and peace within and trust in the evolution of life. Whenever you find yourself in a moment of tension or negative energy, remember that it really isn't that important. There is nothing so fundamental as your connection with the Divine Source within you.

When you experience a rift between you and your beloved, you must make a choice. Nothing is bigger than your love for one another. Take time to centre yourself. Do what you love. Find a way to feel good. Meditate, take a nap, go for a walk or do something else that you enjoy. Don't make it your partner's responsibility to make you happy. Make this commitment to one another; to always find a way to feel good and to not hold them responsible for how you feel. Find your centre of peace and then address whatever has been bothering you both.

Make time to appreciate one another and give thanks for the existence of your beloved in your life. Your relationship will be a pillar of strength; a haven and a space from which you can both create the life of your dreams. Celebrate your love often. Appreciate how lucky you both are and enjoy the expansion, the joy and the creative energy that flows powerfully into your life experience now and forever more.

About the Author

Rachel Blacker is a spiritual teacher and author born in Western Sydney, Australia. Rachel describes her upbringing as 'tumultuous' and 'a smorgasbord of emotions'. Motivated by her challenging childhood, she went on to complete a science degree. During this time, a move to the mountains ignited her passion for the natural environment. When Rachel began working for a large company in her field of expertise, she came to realise that she was not feeling joy in her life and that something had to change.

She decided to embrace her meditation and yoga practice and make changes in her life that were more in alignment with her true values. She sought employment that enabled her to spend more time connecting with nature and the outdoors. Her time spent in the mountains helped to hasten her spiritual awakening and she found comfort in the warm embrace of Mother Nature.

The untimely death of her mother further cemented Rachel's decision to seek meaning beyond the daily grind of full-time work and prompted a move to the coast. Rachel had always felt a pull towards the ocean and in

2011, she moved to the scenic north coast of New South Wales and took up surfing. She hasn't looked back. For Rachel, spending time in nature and in the ocean has been key to her spiritual wellbeing. During her time on the coast, she met her soul mate, Charlie. Together, they have embraced their ideal life, following their intuition at every step. They have spent the last six years travelling together in their beautiful self-built camper van between Charlie's hometown in South Australia and Rachel's adopted home in Northern New South Wales.

Rachel has continued to work on her passions and has completed training in meditation, neuro-linguistic programming, hypnosis and life coaching. Rachel and Charlie continue to work together on their projects, which they hope will improve spiritual wellbeing and appreciation of nature in Western society.

Recommended Resources

Hot Chocolate for the Mystical Soul: 101 True Stories of Miracles, Angels and Healing by Arielle Ford (Thorsons, 1998)

The Power of Now: A Guide to Spiritual Enlightenment by Eckhart Tolle (New World Library, 1999)

Living with Joy: Keys to Personal Power & Spiritual Transformation by Sanaya Roman (HJ Kramer Inc. Publishers, 1986)

Conversations with God: An Uncommon Dialogue by Neale Donald Walsch (Hachette Australia, 1996)

Love Signs: A New Approach to the Human Heart by Linda Goodman (Harper Collins, 2013)

The Law of Attraction: The Basics of the Teachings of Abraham by Esther Hicks & Jerry Hicks (Hay House, 2007)

www.ingramcontent.com/pod-product-compliance
Lightning Source LLC
Chambersburg PA
CBHW010706020526
44107CB00082B/2692